BEHOLD THE WONDER

"Contemplating our Advent and Christmas stories through the original art of Anastassia Cassady and the beautiful writing of Catherine Cavadini opens one's heart, mind, and imagination to a space where scripture comes alive. We are drawn to Mary's trust and wonder and to her magnificent fiat. *Behold the Wonder* invites us to pause, pray, and be intensely present in the quiet places of our own lives."

Marcie Stokman
Founder and President of Well-Read Mom

"*Behold the Wonder* draws you into the heart of Advent through Mary's eyes. It is peaceful, prayerful, and beautiful—a perfect companion to help you notice God's love unfolding in scripture and in your own life."

Erica Tighe Campbell
Founder of Be A Heart and author of *Living the Seasons*

"The Incarnation is the greatest visual event in history. God-made-man, Word-become-flesh is the tangible, visible, knowable mystery that makes up the genetic code of every work of Christian art. Using gentle images to help us recall the humble simplicity of Christ's birth, Cavadini and Cassady invite us to enter into this great and wonderful mystery through prayer, images, scripture, art, and the eyes of the Blessed Mother. *Behold the Wonder* reveals a path for us to live the scriptures of Advent and the early Christmas season more fully and to make their lessons our own."

Elizabeth Lev
Vatican art historian and author of *How Catholic Art Saved the Faith*

"Cavadini and Cassady have written a readily accessible guide for meditating on scripture that will transform your Advent and Christmas. They draw deeply from the wellsprings of Catholic tradition, helping us contemplate the season through Mary's eyes. The images accompanying the text are provocations to prayer showing us the love of Christ made manifest in the Incarnation. The beauty of the art continues in the prose, which often functions as little images for us to wonder at and be renewed by."

Timothy P. O'Malley
Director of Education at the McGrath Institute for Family Life and author of *A Fierce and Tender Love: 7 Meditations on Mary, Mother of God*

BEHOLD THE WONDER

The Coming of Christ Through Mary's Eyes

MEDITATIONS FOR ADVENT AND CHRISTMAS

Catherine Cavadini AND
Anastassia Cassady

Ave Maria Press AVE Notre Dame, Indiana

Nihil Obstat: Reverend Monsignor Michael Heintz, PhD
Censor Librorum
Imprimatur: Most Reverend Kevin C. Rhoades
Bishop of Fort Wayne–South Bend
Given at Fort Wayne, Indiana, on April 29, 2025

Founded in 1865, Ave Maria Press is a ministry of the United States Province of Holy Cross.

www.avemariapress.com

Hardcover: ISBN-13 978-1-64680-401-6

E-book: ISBN-13 978-1-64680-402-3

Cover and text design by Brianna Dombo.

Printed and bound in the United States of America.

Library of Congress Cataloging-in-Publication Data is available.

FOR MY MOTHER, NANCY,
AND MY FATHER, JOHN,
WITH LOVE AND ADMIRATION,
KATIE

FOR MY MOM AND DAD,
WITH GRATITUDE FOR THEIR
DEDICATION TO MY CATECHESIS,
TESS

CONTENTS

INTRODUCTION

Throughout Christian history, in every time and place, the faithful have embraced Mary, the Mother of God and Mother of the Church, with deep gratitude and profound devotion. When studying or reflecting in prayer on biblical accounts of Mary's life, many of us have wondered what she was like, in personality, in character, and—maybe most especially—in her faith. Perhaps you, like me, have imagined her experiences of becoming the Mother of God, giving birth to Jesus, caring for and watching him grow up. Maybe you, too, have wondered what it was like for Mary to speak to the angel Gabriel, to ponder God's Word growing in her womb, and to behold the Divine Wonder cradled in her arms on Christmas morning. Maybe you, too, have contemplated what it was like to bend and kiss the infant Jesus!

Advent is the season for once again kindling our desire to behold God's love in all its magnificent wonder. Nothing but profound love could draw God near enough to become a babe born of a woman and cradled in her arms—a holy child we long to behold and to embrace. The nearer we draw to Christmas, the closer God comes to being with us anew. This book prepares us to contemplate Love, who came to us in the Christ Child long ago at Bethlehem and arrives again each year in the beauty and wonder of Christmas.

MAKING GOOD USE OF THIS BOOK

In the eight meditations of this book, we place our contemplation under Mary's care. She, like us, once longed to behold the one who is God-with-us. She, too, longed for what we now know as Christmas, when we celebrate, contemplate, and seek to share the profound mystery of our salvation in Christ Jesus. As Mary journeyed toward that great day, she, too, grew in faith and understanding of the immense beauty of God's love for each of us and all of us together. We will travel with her as she encounters the angel Gabriel, as she ponders God's love enfleshed within her womb, journeys with Joseph, and beholds her newborn child in the dark of a winter night. As we journey with Mary, she will nurture our desire to see and to respond to God with a humble and open, yes. You see, through the Incarnation, she not only became God's mother, but our mother, too. Her yes to God's love was also a yes to mothering Christ *for us* and *in us*, and for all humankind for all eternity.

PONDERING WITH MARY IN IMAGE AND WORD

Come along as we focus our attention on scripture passages that follow closely the pattern of the readings we hear at Mass each Sunday of Advent; on Christmas Day; on the Solemnity of Mary, Holy Mother of God; and on the Solemnity of the

Epiphany. In the first meditation, however, we reach further back and contemplate the mystery of the annunciation—the moment in time when Mary began her journey as the Mother of God, moving with courage and steadfast faith toward the first Christmas. We celebrate the Solemnity of the Annunciation on March 25 each year, but it is important for our effort in this journey to recall the meaning of this feast as we set out. Because this annunciation meditation is a prologue to our Advent and Christmas meditations, you will want to pray with it either just before Advent begins—perhaps on the Saturday just before the first Sunday of Advent—or on that first Sunday itself. If the latter, you can just keep reading into the second meditation on the first Sunday of Advent, perhaps praying with the annunciation in the morning or early afternoon and praying the meditation for the First Sunday of Advent on Christ Our Hope in the evening of that same day. You choose; there is no right or wrong, better or poorer option here.

With the second meditation, we will settle into the rhythm of walking with Mary week by week according to the Church's calendar and the rhythm of the liturgical season. Meditations 2–5 are for the four weeks of Advent. We will contemplate Christ as Our Hope, Our Peace, Our Joy, and Our Love—one meditation for each week of Advent. In meditations 6–8, for Christmas Day; the Solemnity of Mary, Holy Mother of God; and the Solemnity of the Epiphany, we will settle with our spiritual imaginations into the stable-cave at Bethlehem with Mary and Joseph, deepening our experiences of beholding God's love in and through the Christ Child.

Arising from the scriptural themes we encounter at Mass on the Sundays of Advent and the feasts of the Christmas season are two kinds of prayer that give shape to each of our meditations: *lectio divina,* "divine reading" and *visio divina,* "divine seeing." Together, these two kinds of prayer help us imagine anew scenes from Mary's life and contemplate these scenes with renewed skill for deep sacred reading and spiritually attentive seeing. These two forms of prayer work together here to help us enter into Mary's own experience of beholding and pondering the wondrous mystery of the Incarnation and of bearing and mothering God's love into the world for us and all of humankind.

In the lectio scenes presented for contemplation in this book, scripture is the setting for Mary's thoughts and activities. She remembers, for example, the revelation of God's love throughout the whole of Israel's history; she ponders the prophecies of Isaiah; she wonders at the beauty of God's creation; she longs to kiss her son. The reader, remembering, pondering, and rejoicing with Mary, is brought into the scriptural scene at hand, and is thus drawn closer to beholding her son. In this way, we enter with Mary into the interior spaces of our praying hearts, reaching out for God and desiring to see him as she did.

During the weeks of Advent, you will notice the primary texts for each meditation are from the Old Testament. These are the passages from scripture that Mary would have known, pondered, and prayed with as a first-century Jewish woman. For her, the Hebrew scriptures of the Old Testament were now illuminated by Gabriel's greeting at the annunciation. Each meditation places us alongside Mary as we accompany her through imaginative contemplation. We journey with her in pondering God's Word, in her joyful response to God's activity of love, and in her own beholding of Jesus, the Christ, the Word

Incarnate. At Mary's side and through her eyes, together we behold the wonder.

FORMING THE EYES OF FAITH

Each meditation of *Behold the Wonder* is centered around lectio and visio divina of scripture, and there are six steps to each meditation that guide and support this contemplative Marian journey. Here are some tips for using this book during Advent and the Christmas season to help focus your eyes of faith in order that you might see as Mary saw.

1. Prepare the Way
At the opening of each meditation, we give you a brief introduction or overview of the themes, language, sights, and sounds you will be invited to pray with through the meditation. Think of this as your itinerary.

2. Behold the Word
As you move into the meditation, you will next encounter the passages from scripture that anchors the lectio divina, which in turn, anchors the visio divina. Take your time and read the scripture slowly and prayerfully, noting the words or phrases that stand out to you, that speak to you, or that take on Marian qualities. After reading the scripture passages, move on to the guide for entering into both the lectio and visio prayers of the meditation.

3. Consider the Scene

In order to cultivate our capacities for these types of prayer, we include a simple guide for you, rooted in the scriptures of each meditation. The purpose of the guide is twofold. First, the guide will help you plumb the beautiful depths of our Tradition, from ancient scriptural commentaries to current holiday observances, all of which help one approach Mary and Jesus as we pray. For more than two thousand years now, the Church has been contemplating the mystery of the Incarnation and responding with heart, mind, and soul. When we listen, gaze, and behold with Mary, we do so with the whole Tradition, the whole Church.

The second purpose of the guide in each meditation is to help all of us not only receive the beauty of our Tradition, and join its chorus, but to assist us in handing on our faith to others. Perhaps Mary will guide us toward new prayerful experiences of hearing and seeing our gracious God and always knowing how to behold his love.

4. Pray with Lectio Divina

When you are ready, move on to the lectio divina by entering prayerfully into the story presented in this step, rooted in the scripture passages of each meditation. Each pertinent scripture passage appears in italics so that you can see which words and phrases stand out to us (authors Catherine and Anastassia) as having Marian qualities as we pondered the scriptures. These are the words and phrases that spoke to us most powerfully, as Catherine wrote the story and Anastassia created the art with which you will pray in the next step. Let the story open wide your eyes, your heart, and your imagination to Mary and to her love for her son, Jesus.

5. Contemplate with Visio Divina

When you are ready, move on to the visio, which has been thoughtfully and prayerfully composed as an entry point into Mary's own contemplative gaze. Spending time with the images in prayer will allow Mary to form your gazing, too. As you look, take note of the things within the image that catch your attention. What do you notice first, and why? Let your eyes wander over the whole image. Take in every detail. As you become aware of what you are responding to in the image—the emotions and insights that present themselves—you will be walking with Mary toward Christmas.

Each image you encounter is also part of the story told by the lectio divina. Thus, as you gaze and pray during the visio divina, you will be drawn to return to the story of the lectio divina to reread it in its entirety or return to specific parts of it as you continue to gaze and pray in visio divina. Please note that there is no right or wrong way to pray here.

6. Follow Mary Today

Each meditation concludes with a story from the lives of saints who help us follow Mary today. The saint chosen for each week witnesses to and exemplifies the same dispositions of faith and love that we discover in the scripture, journeying with Mary, and that we seek to imitate, especially during Advent.

BEHOLD YOUR MOTHER

The stories and images in this book are not meant to be wooden or stiff, nor are they exhaustive. Rather, they are offered to you as a beginning. We hope they will inspire deeper prayer and greater rejoicing at the thought of God's love for us and his never faltering presence among us. May Mary become the mother of all our beholding of wonder during this holy season and always. And may she bring forth and mother a vision of God's love within our hearts. Walk alongside Mary. See through her eyes the wonder of love before us. She will prepare you to behold her son in majesty, peace, and joyful hope on Christmas morning and beyond.

If we follow Mary into the story of the Gospel from the moment of the annunciation until Christ's birth and the manifestation of who he is, we encounter a whole chorus of believers saying, "Rejoice . . . Yes!" By the time we arrive at Epiphany, the Magi will have come with great joy and rejoiced exceedingly at the sight of the newborn king. The further we enter into the story of the Incarnation, the more our joy grows, for we truly come to know God's love by contemplating it under Mary's mantle and beholding the mystery of love through Mary's eyes.

ONE

BEHOLD THE INCARNATION

AS ADVENT BEGINS

PREPARE THE WAY

For as long as the Church has prayed the "Hail Mary," we have contemplated the Incarnation through this greeting, and so through Mary at the annunciation when the angel Gabriel first made known the Father's plan. The words "Hail Mary" could be more literally translated as "Rejoice, Mary!" The first word of Luke's gospel, spoken by the angel Gabriel, is a tiding of joy. Through the joyful tidings of the annunciation, Mary draws the faithful to Christ, who is the very Love of God, enfleshed for us.

In the fourteenth century, the Feast of the Annunciation even marked the beginning of the New Year. All time was measured "from the Incarnation," and every year began by joyfully remembering the unique moment in our history when God became one of us. The Incarnation is the moment when God fully unveiled his love for us. From that time forward, all people could behold his love in flesh, word, and deed. Celebrating and remembering the annunciation forms our hearts to see the Father's love, made flesh in Jesus, always and everywhere.

As our new liturgical year starts with the First Sunday of Advent, we begin our journey toward Christmas by imagining the annunciation. We place ourselves next to Mary as the angel comes to her and says, "Rejoice!" To behold Mary in this moment is to glimpse Christ for the first time. We begin to see God's great love for us through the mystery of the Incarnation from the very moment it was announced. From this joy-filled beginning, we will journey with Mary toward a fuller and fuller vision of God's love until we behold the child Jesus himself.

May the art and story of this lectio and visio divina kindle our desire for such wondrous beholding. May Gabriel's bidding to rejoice fill and direct our hearts as we journey with Mary on her Advent journey. May her response, "Yes! Let it be done unto me," help prepare the eyes of our hearts for a rapturous moment of beholding the Love of God in the Christ Child at Christmas.

BEHOLD THE WORD

LUKE 1:26–38

In the sixth month the angel Gabriel was sent from God to a city of Galilee named Nazareth, to a virgin betrothed to a man whose name was Joseph, of the house of David; and the virgin's name was Mary. And he came to her and said, "Hail, full of grace, the Lord is with you!" But she was greatly troubled at the saying, and considered in her mind what sort of greeting this might be. And the angel said to her, "Do not be afraid, Mary, for you have found favor with God. And behold, you will conceive in your womb and bear a son, and you shall call his name Jesus.

He will be great, and will be called the Son of the Most High;
and the Lord God will give to him the throne of his father David,
and he will reign over the house of Jacob forever;
and of his kingdom there will be no end."

And Mary said to the angel, "How can this be, since I have no husband?" And the angel said to her,

"The Holy Spirit will come upon you,
and the power of the Most High will overshadow you;
therefore the child to be born will be called holy,
the Son of God.

And behold, your kinswoman Elizabeth in her old age has also conceived a son; and this is the sixth month with her who was called barren. For with God nothing will be impossible." And Mary said, "Behold, I am the handmaid of the Lord; let it be to me according to your word." And the angel departed from her.

CONSIDER THE SCENE

Have you ever tried to imagine the moment of the Incarnation? Where was Mary? What was she doing? What would it have been like to encounter an archangel? Or even just to hear the voice of the angel speaking to her? Only the evangelist Luke recounts the annunciation, and he doesn't tell us any of these details. But we can look for them elsewhere in scripture and in the life of the Church!

When trying to envision the scene of the annunciation, the Church has imagined Mary busy with different tasks: spinning thread for the temple veil, drawing water from a well, and reading the scriptures, often in a garden. We imagined all three in our lectio! All are anchored, however, in the third task: Mary's contemplation of the scriptures. When the angel Gabriel arrives, Tradition describes Mary as reading either Psalm 45:10, with which our lectio divina begins, or Isaiah 7:14, with which our lectio divina ends.

Psalm 45:10 reads: "Hear, O daughter, consider and incline your ear, forget your people and your father's house; and the king will desire your beauty." This is just what Mary is doing when the angel Gabriel arrives: "pondering," as Luke will put it, or, here in the psalm, "inclining her ear" to God's Word. The Tradition often thinks of Mary as "conceiving" Christ first through her ear, and then in her mind in faith. In this way, the psalm text becomes a description of Mary herself, desired by God for the beauty of her faith, as soon as Gabriel announces the good news.

A GARDEN IN BLOOM

Moving further into Luke's narrative of the annunciation, we find plenty of imaginative space in scripture for developing his sparse scene. Much of this space can be discovered in Mary's own pondering. She is listening, almost waiting at every moment for God to speak! Her listening to God comes before her seeing of God. This is because seeing God is the result of Mary's yes to the Incarnation. With the Church, we imagine Mary's obedient yes in contrast to Eve's disobedient no in the Garden of Eden. Obedience involves listening. Both Eve and Mary are asked to listen and respond to God's self-revelation. Unlike Eve's (and Adam's) no, Mary's yes responds to God's revelation of love. Yes: "I receive and I respond to Divine Love, with the whole of myself!"

With the help of scripture, we also imagine the annunciation taking place in a garden full of flowers. Nearly every depiction of the annunciation imagined by the Church includes flowers. If the scene is not a garden proper, there is a vase or a pitcher placed between Mary and the angel, and usually it is full of white lilies. The Song of Solomon is a scriptural text that describes the annunciation by way of flowers: "flowers appear on the earth . . . and the voice of the turtledove is heard in our land" (Sg 2:12). We take up this allegory in our lectio.

With Mary's yes, the flowers of Israel bloom. With Mary's yes, she mothers God's love into the world. The life that is God and that God alone can give to us is experienced by Mary at the annunciation. And the fruitfulness of divine life is imaged in her garden full of flowers during springtime. We imagine the various flowers of the land of Israel, many of which are mentioned by name throughout the Song of Solomon. The wind sweeping across a fiery field of springtime flowers hints to us of the presence of the Holy Spirit who overshadows Mary at the annunciation, and who enflames all of us with love for God.

THE INCARNATION AS HISTORY

Yet these flowers are not just an imaginative allegory, but evidence that the Incarnation was a real historical event. This is one of the joys of the Gospel, which offers us good reason to believe that God truly became human in a particular place and time. God truly loves us that much. And so, the flowers of Israel locate the annunciation in its particular time and place within human history. St. Bernard of Clairvaux once imagined the particular moment of the Incarnation. We read what he imagined during Advent, in the Office of Readings for December 20. In his imaginative homily, Bernard describes the whole world as holding its breath as it awaits Mary's response to the angel: "You have heard, O Virgin," Bernard writes, "that you will conceive and bear a son; you have heard that it will not be by man but by the Holy Spirit . . . We too are waiting, O Lady . . ."[1]

Yes, we are waiting, and we all need Mary to say yes. Our lectio echoes St. Bernard's vision. Here, the breathless waiting of the faithful is captured by the garden's stillness. Indeed, all in Nazareth is still and hanging on this expectant moment. Even the flowers seem to lean in and wait for Mary to reply.

GABRIEL

Pope Benedict XVI describes the voice of the angels as being like a song. And since we don't have much experience of the angels, singing seems an appropriate way for us to imagine Gabriel, especially when delivering the first word of the Gospel, "Hail!" or "Rejoice!"

THE HOLY SPIRIT

The final bit of imagining concerns the moment after Mary says yes. What was it like to be overshadowed by the Holy Spirit? Here, we imagine with the poetic images of light and water in John's gospel. At the annunciation, Mary becomes the Mother of the One who *is* the light and water we need. God's love is our bread and drink. Mary drinks of this water at the annunciation, and her soul is filled with the light that is Christ.

This leads our imaginations to one further revelation: God also drinks in the moment of the Incarnation. As Psalm 45 told Mary (and all of us) at the beginning of our lectio, God desires our beauty. God desires to embrace us and to be with us! And now, through Mary, God has done so.

PRAY WITH LECTIO DIVINA

Morning sunshine spills through Mary's window, illuminating the psalm spread across her lap. She reads aloud, to no one in particular, for the house is empty.

> Hear, O daughter, consider, and incline your ear;
> forget your people and your father's house;
> and the king will desire your beauty. (Ps 45:10–11)

Mary sets the scriptures aside, eyes the crimson thread wound round her spindle, and listens. She considers a humming sound, coming and going just outside her window: bees, busy in the sun-warmed blossoms. Spiny broom flower, despite its prickly name, warms the landscape with brilliant yellow blossoms. Red, papery poppies bob and bounce under the weight of tiny bee bodies, fanning the yellow-laden fields into flowered-flames. Here and there, an iris stands tall and purple. Somewhere hidden in the cypress, the flowers become honey.

Mary hears the wind, too, just outside her window. Sweeping across the fiery fields with a whisper; the wind rushes inside to announce the fragrant presence of blue hyacinth, narcissus, and the lily of the valley. It is springtime in Nazareth: *flowers appear on the earth . . . and the voice of the turtledove is heard in our land* (Sg 2:12). And then, as if on cue, Mary hears the singsong sound of the wind swinging the dipper that hangs from the garden well. She will go out and make that song into her morning drink.

But as Mary steps into the garden, all is strangely still. The bees are no longer humming. And all the garden looks as though it has been drawn, as Mary is, to the garden well.

Perhaps the lilies, and the tall irises, and the spiny broom flowers were swept that way by the wind? Or, perhaps they, too, are thirsty for a morning drink?

Mary drops the dipper in, splashing golden sunlight into the grass. And then, as she watches the light dance across the water's surface, she hears a voice, melodious and beautiful.

"Rejoice! Hail!"

No wonder the light and water dance together! But Mary stands and listens, her head inclined toward the angel's melody.

"Rejoice, Mary, full of grace. The Lord is with you."

Leaning even further in, Mary wonders. "What sort of greeting is this?" She remembers the psalm that sprawled across her lap just moments earlier: "Hear, O daughter, consider, and incline your ear . . ."

> *Do not be afraid, Mary, for you have found favor with God. And behold, you will conceive in your womb and bear a son, and you shall call his name Jesus. He will be great, and will be called the Son of the Most High; and the Lord God will give to him the throne of his father David, and he will reign over the house of Jacob forever; and of his kingdom there will be no end.* (Lk 1:30–33)

Not only is the garden still, but so now is the world beyond its walls. Yet the angel has spoken his song. What will Mary say in response? She stands at the well, her wonder deepening. "How will this be, since I do not have a husband?" (Lk 1:34). Her soul seeks to make sense of the angel's words as they converge with the feeling of joy that has taken hold of her soul, flowing through her like water and light: ". . . The king will desire your beauty . . ."

> *The Holy Spirit will come upon you, and the power of the Most High will overshadow you; therefore the child to be born will be called holy, the Son of God.* (Lk 1:35)

> *Then Mary said, "Behold, I am the handmaid of the Lord; let it be to me according to your word."* (Lk 1:38)

> *"Behold, a virgin shall conceive and bear a son, and shall call his name Imman'u-el."* (Is 7:14)

CONTEMPLATE WITH VISIO DIVINA

Gaze at this painting for a few minutes. What catches your attention? What do you notice first, and why? Take in every detail—the colors, light, depiction of the created world. What emotions and insights well up in you?

FOLLOW MARY TODAY

Servant of God Takashi Nagai lay dying in Nagasaki. It was September of 1945, and the world around him was devastated by the atomic bomb. A doctor himself, Nagai tells us that he knew he was dying. He was aware of the slowing of his pulse.

Nagai's friends who were attending to him were all doctors and nurses he had worked with at the hospital. They, too, knew he was dying, and at the moment of death, even. They poured a drop of Lourdes water into his mouth and told him to pray to Our Lady and St. Maximilian Kolbe. Nagai tells us what happened next.

> Between half-closed eyelids, I saw the roses in bloom of that grotto of Lourdes and the radiant image of the Immaculate Virgin . . . I said in prayer, 'may it happen according to [God's] will,' and I opened my mouth. Like a flow of water from a turbine, I felt the water of Lourdes flowing through my dying body . . . [2]

Nagai felt love and life coursing through his veins. His own description of this miracle—of feeling life flowing back into his dying body—can help us to think about the moment of the annunciation. Not in the sense that Mary needed life to flow again through her immaculate self, but that there was a particular moment in our history in which the Incarnation happened. Mary, with all the freedom of grace, offered herself as the mother necessary for the Incarnation. In this way, Mary, with God's grace, helps to pour the divine life out upon us all.

We, too, can receive that life that is love. Divine love can course through us like "a spring of water welling up to eternal life" (see John 4:14), or like light flooding through a window and coursing into our souls. These are images of salvation offered to us by the Incarnation. We just need to say a bold and trusting yes, as did Mary, to the God who perfectly loves us.

TWO

BEHOLD CHRIST OUR HOPE

FIRST SUNDAY OF ADVENT

PREPARE THE WAY

During the first Advent, Mary carried the hope of Israel in her womb. Her son, the very one who is our hope because he is "God with us," *Immanuel*, was hidden silently within her. Once born, Mary's son would speak the Good News with his own lips. But until then, it was only the angel Gabriel's joyful "Hail!" that illuminated Mary's heart as she contemplated God's hope-filled promises of old, which she knew from the Hebrew scriptures.

Our own hope, like Mary's hope, is a response to the hope of new life given to us in Jesus. Mary's hope orients us toward a new life with God, though hope also fills our journey with his presence here and now, day by day. We begin to see the presence of God's love all around us—to see the light *coming into the world*. With Mary, we begin to see something so wondrous that we could not have imagined it for ourselves. Indeed, as Isaiah declared: *From of old no one has heard or perceived by the ear, no eye has seen a God besides you, who works for those who wait for him* (Is 64:4).

The visio and lectio divina for the first Sunday of Advent imagine Mary observing the very light that illuminates the world around her. Mary's hope, anchored in the angel's greeting, encourages her to look for God's light made visible around her as it is being made visible within her. The child in her womb then takes hold of her hope, handed down from her ancestors *of old*, and transforms it in his light. For Mary, the whole world has grown luminous. All things are hope filled and light soaked!

As we light the first Advent candle, may Mary ignite our hope and shine the light of Christ upon our Advent journey toward Christmas Day.

BEHOLD THE WORD

ISAIAH 2:2–3, 5

It shall come to pass in the latter days
that the mountain of the house of the LORD
shall be established as the highest of the mountains,
and shall be raised above the hills;
and all the nations shall flow to it,
and many peoples shall come, and say:
"Come, let us go up to the mountain of the LORD,
to the house of the God of Jacob;
that he may teach us his ways

and that we may walk in his paths."
For out of Zion shall go forth the law,
and the word of the LORD from Jerusalem.
O house of Jacob,
come, let us walk
in the light of the LORD.

ISAIAH 64:1–4

O that you would tear the heavens and come down,
that the mountains might quake at your presence—
as when fire kindles brushwood
and the fire causes water to boil—
to make your name known to your adversaries,
and that the nations might tremble at your presence!
When you did terrible things which we looked not for,
you came down, the mountains quaked at your presence.
From of old no one has heard
or perceived by the ear,
no eye has seen a God besides you,
who works for those who wait for him.

CONSIDER THE SCENE

Our light-filled scene depicts Mary journeying home from Elizabeth's house, through the hills of Judea and then the fields of the Jezreel Valley. Surrounded by light, Mary remembers Elizabeth greeting her as the "Mother of my Lord." With Mary, Elizabeth delighted in the fulfilment of Israel's hope—and ours!

The women together delighted in the one who is Immanuel, "God with us." And now we are to join them with delight!

SEEING LIGHT UNDER A MARIAN SKY

Mary invites the whole house of Israel to walk with her in the light of the Lord. As we go with Mary, she prepares our eyes for that which eye has not seen, nor ear heard, but for which the human heart has hoped. In his gospel, John describes "the light coming into the world." In our lectio, Mary, our guide, becomes our lens for seeing Christ as light, streaming all around us.

This was true for Mary's cousin, Elizabeth. Her sight—formed by Mary's good news—saw what cannot be seen directly. Elizabeth recognized God's presence within Mary, calling Mary the "mother of [her] Lord" (see Luke 1:43). Elizabeth understood that Mary was bringing the Light, who is Christ, into the world.

Trying to capture the same idea of Mary making God visible to us, the Jesuit poet Gerard Manley Hopkins compares Mary to the sky. It is a helpful comparison: We only see the sky because the sunlight streams through it. The sunlight makes the sky a beautiful blue! And that beautiful blue becomes a way of beholding the light as it comes into the world. Hopkins puts it more poetically, writing:

> How air is azurèd . . .
> The glass-blue days are those
> When every color glows,
> Each shape and shadow shows.
> Blue be it: this blue heaven
> The seven or seven times seven
> Hued sunbeam will transmit
> Perfect, not alter it.[1]

Ah! Yes, Mary is our sky! She is a glass-blue day, for she alone transmits the Light that is Christ, as it appeared on our horizon. She "let all God's glory through."[2] Mary is the one through whom *what no eye has seen* is offered to our sight.

In our lectio, you will encounter Mary tracing the presence of the sunlight as it moves over the Judean Hills and through the Jezreel Valley, from the sky and the hills at sunrise, to the contours of Mt. Tabor, to the harvest-ready wheat and the watermelons of the field.

AWESOME DEEDS

Beholding the sunlight this way with Mary, we enter into her own prayerful reflection on God's awesome deeds of old. Remember, Mary would not have read the New Testament. She has, rather, the greeting of the angel, the child in her womb, and the hopes of her ancestors as retold in Israel's scriptures. Those ancient hopes are transfigured now by the angel and her child. Her ear has heard *what no eye has seen*. Our Advent journey begins with a unique Marian vantage point of view—contemplating the light of Christ *coming into the world*.

POETIC ROOTS

Mary's unique relationship to the Old Testament inspires us to look at the poetry of St. Ephrem (d. 373), who wrote many beautiful hymns filled with imagery from the Hebrew scriptures. In his hymns on the Nativity, St. Ephrem imagines the prophecies of old, like Isaiah's prophecy, finding their final fulfilment in Mary's flesh and writes from her perspective.

> "I, [Mary], became a haven for Your sake,
> great Sea. Behold, the psalms

of Your father David and also the words
of the prophets, like ships
discharge in me Your great wealth."[3]

St. Ephrem honors Mary for making God visible to us according to God's promises; according to that in which Israel hoped!

Ephrem poetically calls Mary our "eye." "Behold the world!" he writes. "To it were given two eyes: Eve was the left eye, the blind eye; the right eye, the luminous eye, is Mary . . ."[4] And when "the world once more begins to shine," says Ephrem, it will shine with "the light of heaven," come to dwell within Mary.

And so, let us draw near to Mary as we begin our Advent journey, such that each day of this Season and each step of our journey brings us closer to beholding Christ, the Light of the Glass-Blue Sky, and the very vision of our hope fulfilled.

PRAY WITH LECTIO DIVINA

Mary [had] remained with [Elizabeth] about three months (see Luke 1:56). It was time for the long journey home from the Judean hills to Nazareth. On her journey into the hill country, the words of Isaiah had been Mary's prayer, "O house of Jacob, come, let us walk in the light of the LORD" (see Isaiah 2:5). Mary arrived at Elizabeth's home, radiant and quick to embrace her cousin. With great delight, Elizabeth let Mary's happiness stream over and through her, as *the child in her womb leaped for joy!* And now, the same words of Isaiah and the same steady joy of hopes fulfilled would again be Mary's prayer on her journey home: *Come, let us walk!*

Ever since the sunlight had spilled from the garden well and the melodious "Rejoice" had entered her soul, Mary had found the Lord's light everywhere. The whole world had become an annunciation! Light welled up and spilled from all things.

On the morning that she had set out to visit Elizabeth, Mary had stepped beyond the rose-laden wall of the garden into the light-soaked world around her: Sunlight filled the Jezreel Valley. Mary had watched the sunlight, pale pink and tipped with gold, surround Mt. Tabor to the east, push over the solitary mountain, and spread a hundred hues of violet-red across the morning sky. As the sun rose higher, the valley brimmed with blue. The light settled in and spread out between tree and flower, all the way to Mt. Carmel, to the west.

Today, too, as she headed north, the morning light encircled the hills and illuminated a symphony of greens: in grass and trees, in new growth and old. *No one has heard or perceived by the ear, no eye has seen, a God besides you* working such wonders *for those who wait for him* (Is 64:4). *What no eye has seen* was now the secret of her womb, announcing himself to her, to Elizabeth, and soon to all. Isaiah's words accompanied Mary as she set off northward through the hills and toward the Jezreel Valley: *Oh, that you would tear the heavens and come down,* with the mountains quaking before you, while you work awesome deeds that we could not have hoped for, such as they had not heard of *from of old* (see Isaiah 64:1, 3–4).

Leaving the hills behind, fields soon stretched in every direction. Wheat fields, once grass-green, grew golden. The light now held within the grain, stored up day by day, would soon be their bread. Melon patches swelled alongside the wheat. The viny plants curled their way through the dark soil, wending themselves hopefully to the edge of Mary's path. Like the grains of wheat, the melons grew plump and plentiful. The pale pink of the sunrise was now hidden within each one, richly red. *Of old*, Mary knew, her ancestors had crossed the Egyptian desert, sustained by God's wondrous deeds, yet pining for melons (see Numbers 11:5).

> "O house of Jacob," Mary prayed, step by step, "come,
> let us walk in the light of the Lord!"

Of old, the light of the Lord had poured forth God's awesome deeds: pillars of fire; a wind sweeping the sea into dry land; manna from heaven. And yet, looking about her, Mary knew that somehow our human hearts hoped for something smaller, something more familiar. The black seed of a watermelon, a new shoot peeking from dry earth, perhaps a loaf of hearth-baked bread.

And now God had rent *the heavens and come down*! The sunlight streaming round, between tree and flower and wending watermelon, was not simply a great star's light. The light streaming from the heavens now colored and contoured a new vision of God's most awesome deed—one *no ear has heard, no eye has seen*! This awesome deed was something smaller, something more familiar. Hidden in Mary's womb, a shoot was sprouting. Hidden in Mary's breast, a pillar of fire was illuminating every human heart. And soon a child would give them bread, such as they had not heard of *from of old*.

Elizabeth's voice came back to Mary, from amidst the greens and blues, the violet and the gold, and the black seeds of the ripening melons: "Blessed are you among women, and blessed is the fruit of your womb!" (Lk 1:42). The joyful feeling of flowing light in her soul coursed through her again as Mary hurried on, passing fields of sunflowers, tall and turned toward the sun. Joseph would be waiting.

CONTEMPLATE WITH VISIO DIVINA

Gaze at this painting for a few minutes. What things catch your attention? What do you notice first, and why? Take in every detail—the colors, light, depiction of the created world. What emotions and insights well up in you?

FOLLOW MARY TODAY

When St. Laura Montoya (d. 1949) was just eight years old, she spent much of her time alone. There were two daily activities that she loved: praying the Rosary with her family and spending time outdoors. One morning, a particularly busy anthill caught little Laura's attention. She was entranced by these tiny insects and watched them with great curiosity as they carried leaves from nearby trees, across the field and down into the sandy anthill and the dark soil below.

St. Laura remembered that morning as a mystical experience later in life, and described its effect on her soul: "It was as if I were struck by a lightning bolt; it was a knowledge of God and his grandeurs, so profound, so magnificent and so loving . . ."[5]

Perhaps "Mother Mary," as St. Laura called her, helped Laura to see the grandeur of God in the tiniest of creatures. God's love struck like lightning and illuminated all things with its light. To pray the Rosary is to gaze meditatively upon the Incarnation with Mary. In this way, Mary helps us to see God's love made visible in all the things of day-to-day life. Even the ant, as St. Laura observed, has life through God's love, and we can contemplate that love with great hope when Mary is by our side, journeying with us: *Hail Mary, full of grace, the Lord is with thee . . .*

THREE

BEHOLD CHRIST OUR PEACE

SECOND SUNDAY OF ADVENT

PREPARE THE WAY

We continue our Advent journey with Mary this week by contemplating Christ as our peace. Mary—full of grace—knows the peace the human heart truly seeks. She alone, in her response to the angel Gabriel, has given her whole self over to bring Christ, who is peace, into the world. Mary guides us to recognize divine peace in the face of her son on Christmas morning.

Contemplating Christ with Mary, we glimpse Mary's peace: her heart at rest in God's love, giving everything and responding to the deepest of human desires. The heart that knows God's peace-filled rest communicates the comfort of a tenderness beyond our understanding. In our visio and lectio divina for this week, Mary embodies this tenderness by descending into the sorrows of a small boy, not unlike her own son, and mothering God's peace within the small boy's heart. She seeks to swaddle him with a story of God's love—with, that is, the story of her son, swaddled now in her womb, but a story soon to be made known to all by an infant's face.

Keeping our gaze upon Mary this week, may she continue to lead us to the peace of Christmas, not only through the prophetic stories of Christ's coming, but, soon, by the very visage of her son.

BEHOLD THE WORD

ISAIAH 11:1–10

There shall come forth a shoot from the stump of Jesse,
and a branch shall grow out of his roots.
And the Spirit of the LORD shall rest upon him,
the spirit of wisdom and understanding,
the spirit of counsel and might,
the spirit of knowledge and the fear of the LORD.
And his delight shall be in the fear of the LORD.

He shall not judge by what his eyes see,
or decide by what his ears hear;
but with righteousness he shall judge the poor,
and decide with equity for the meek of the earth;
and he shall strike the earth with the rod of his mouth,
and with the breath of his lips he shall slay the wicked.

Righteousness shall be the belt of his waist,
and faithfulness the belt of his loins.

The wolf shall dwell with the lamb,
and the leopard shall lie down with the kid,
and the calf and the lion and the fatling together,
and a little child shall lead them.
The cow and the bear shall feed;
their young shall lie down together;
and the lion shall eat straw like the ox.
The sucking child shall play over the hole of the asp,
and the weaned child shall put his hand on the adder's den.
They shall not hurt or destroy
in all my holy mountain;
for the earth shall be full of the knowledge of the LORD
as the waters cover the sea.

In that day the root of Jesse shall stand as an ensign to the peoples; him shall the nations seek, and his dwellings shall be glorious.

ISAIAH 40:1–2, 9–11

Comfort, comfort my people,
says your God.
Speak tenderly to Jerusalem,
and cry to her
that her warfare is ended,
that her iniquity is pardoned,
that she has received from the LORD*'s hand*
double for all her sins.

Get you up to a high mountain,
O Zion, herald of good tidings;
lift up your voice with strength,
O Jerusalem, herald of good tidings,
lift it up, fear not;
say to the cities of Judah,
"Behold your God!"
Behold, the Lord God comes with might,
and his arm rules for him;
behold, his reward is with him,
and his recompense before him.
He will feed his flock like a shepherd,
he will gather the lambs in his arms,
he will carry them in his bosom,
and gently lead those that are with young.

CONSIDER THE SCENE

Peace! St. Augustine once described peace as rest. Our hearts, he says, are restless until they rest in God. The peace of Christmas is this rest, and the Christ Child is the Prince of Peace. He truly is Immanuel, reconciling us with God by coming to dwell with us. One day soon, we will be able to rest our heads upon his breast (see John 13:23).

PEACE AND REST

We all know the feeling of unrest, of peace with God being disrupted by sin. It is surely the opposite of comfort, of tenderness. As did Mary in the marketplace of Nazareth, we move between these feelings of unrest and feelings of comforting tenderness. After last week's effort to see the Christ Light streaming all around, we are asked now to also recognize the absence of light: the darkness of sin. In our hope, we seek the comfort of being at peace, at rest, with God.

And so, we go with Mary into the marketplace of Nazareth, into a scene woven from the language of our fall in Genesis 2 and 3, but also illuminated by Mary's tender and loving comfort.

In this imaginative scene, the images of thorns and thistles, of dust and toil and sweat, are lifted from Genesis 3:17–19, where Adam and Eve (and we, too!) confront the consequences of sin: *In the sweat of your face you shall eat bread till you return to the ground, for out of it you were taken; you are dust and to dust you shall return* (Gn 3:19).

IMAGES OF SIN

But what is the sin of Adam and Eve? Sometimes sin is hard to see. It is but a shadow, a darkness, an absence of love and goodness. In short, the sin of Adam and Eve is our sin also; it is the sin of all humanity, a turning away from God in pride, with the ungrateful declaration: "I don't need you!"

Instead of expressing gratitude for the gift of life, we so often wish to be self-sufficient, to be as gods for ourselves. Through sin much unrest enters into the world, bringing with it thorns and thistles and shadowy, dusty darkness.

In our lectio this week, original sin is not only represented by dust and thorns, but also by King Herod's coins. Herod's coins were a way for Herod to exercise dominion over Israel, a dominion by which Herod suggested he was god, a dominion under which many in Israel suffered poverty and great indignity. Herod's coins further illuminate the sin of Adam and Eve as a commerce. Adam, Eve, and the serpent each put something into a common purse and sinned together. The serpent, a medieval monk's commentary says, contributed his teeth!

Returning to the marketplace with Mary, we encounter the extent of the whole brambly hedge of thorns and thistles of sin from which it is impossible to escape, except by God's love. Mary initiates a new commerce in the marketplace: that of God's gratuitous love!

MARY: COMFORT AMIDST THE MARKET

Unnoticed in the dusty shadows of the street, Mary buys fruit and bread to share with the small boy, transforming Herod's coin into a gift of bread, of comfort, and of rest. In the gospels, Christ will call such gifts works of mercy. With Mary's gifts, we behold, and we receive love, as does the small boy.

Mary comforts the boy in the marketplace with a story about the *Prince of Peace*, preparing his heart, and ours, for God's love. As Mary tells this story, she sees the face of her unborn babe in the face of this child in the marketplace. Now this boy, too, with Mary, and with all of us, can look forward to the marvelous day when the Prince of Peace will dispel our darkness.

PRAY WITH LECTIO DIVINA

"Herod the Tetrarch." Mary turned the small bronze coin over in her hand. On the reverse, a palm wreath glinted dully, surrounding the Roman word Mary had come to recognize as "Tiberius." So many in Nazareth and throughout all of Galilee took *comfort* in the weight of these foreign coins in their hands. And why shouldn't they? They were the currency of the empire! But at tax time, Herod would hold open his own hands and leave them open until the hands of the poor were empty. In truth, these coins did not represent *comfort*, but toil, sweat, pain, and the warring of human hearts over the dust of the earth. Since Adam, such toil, sweat, and pain were the thorns of sin (see Genesis 3:18–19); they were the teeth of the serpent upon Eve's heel. And it was the poor who felt the keenest bite.

Mary placed a coin in the coarse hand of an aged woman selling hearth cakes at the market. A second coin bought a ripe pomegranate and some figs. At the edge of the market, Mary noticed a small boy. He sat alone, sunken beneath the clouds of dust and the long shadows of the passersby. Without a single word, his whole being cried out to Mary: Who will notice my hunger? My thirst? My lonely, thorn-pricked heart? Watching the boy, the words of Isaiah welled up in Mary: *Comfort, O comfort, my people!* She stepped into the dusty shadows, and bent low to sit with him.

Mary broke her hearth cake in two, but what she handed him was not just a morsel of bread, but the comfort of being noticed and cared for. He needed so much more than a morsel of bread! She decided to share a story with him, like the stories her parents shared with her when she was a small girl. The nourishing words of Isaiah seemed just right. Mary *spoke tenderly* to him while the marketplace bustled on with its business. She told the boy a story of a small *Prince* who was just like him. She carried this story in her heart always, and knew it well. Mary told her story to the little boy—who was now savoring her half of the hearth cake—in these words:

Soon a little boy, just like you, will be born. He will be called the Prince of Peace, and he will be filled with *the spirit of the*

Lord! When he comes, we will know him by his love, for his love will do marvelous things.

In Israel, there was once a magnificent tree. All the birds lived in its branches until pride cut it down. The little Prince of Peace will love Israel and all the world so completely, that this magnificent tree, now only a dead *stump*, will come back to life! At first, just a small sprout will spring up: a twig and a few green leaves. But as the tree grows, the stump will *branch out* and become more magnificent than ever before. It will be a Living Tree, so tall and full of life that the Prince's whole kingdom will come and live under its branches. The young and old, the rich and poor, will rest together in the Tree's shade and eat its healing fruit (see Isaiah 11, Revelation 22, Ezekiel 17, and Matthew 13). And when that happens, we will all see this small prince's love do other even more marvelous things, too:

> "The wolf," Mary continued, "shall live with the lamb;
> the leopard shall lie down with the kid;
> the calf and the lion will feed together;
> and a little child shall lead them.
> The cow and the bear shall graze;
> their young shall lie down together;
> and the lion shall eat straw like the ox . . ."

Already, there in the marketplace, a marvelous thing was happening: The boy smiled and, without a single word, took Mary's hand in his, happily aware of God's tender love. Mary smiled, too, and knew that soon and very soon . . . a boy, much like the little boy sitting next to her, was coming into the world, and that he would be our *Prince of Peace* (see Isaiah 9:6).

CONTEMPLATE WITH VISIO DIVINA

Gaze at this painting for a few minutes. What things catch your attention? What do you notice first, and why? Take in every detail—the colors, light, depiction of the created world. What emotions and insights well up in you?

FOLLOWING MARY TODAY

The martyrs and confessors of Tsuwano, Japan, are fitting company as we contemplate Mary as the mother of peace. The martyrs and confessors of Tsuwano suffered many thorns of sin at the hands of their persecutors. Two friends, Jinzaburo and Yasutaro, give us a window into the Mary-like faith of these peaceful witnesses to God's love.

Yasutaro loved Mary, and he prayed to her often, seeking her comfort. Jinzaburo tells us of a moment of great comfort offered to Yasutaro by Mary herself. In late March of 1869, Yasutaro, a humble man, was imprisoned in a cage of three *saku* (three square meters) in size. He could not stand up straight, nor could he sit or lay down! It was exhausting. Not only was Yasutaro confined to this cage of three *saku*, but he was also immersed, while in his cage, in the deep snows of the Japanese winter.

Jinzaburo, desiring to comfort his friend, no matter what it might cost him, dug a hole through the icy snow to a place near enough Yasutaro's cage to call his name: "Yasutaro! Yasutaro!" At first Jinzaburo only heard the silence of the snow. But then Yasutaro responded softly to Jinzaburo's call.

"[Yasutaro] answered that . . . he was not alone at all because every day, starting at midnight, a woman dressed in a blue dress and with a veil of the same color, whose face resembled that of Saint Mary, came to visit him and kept him company with her stories until the early hours of the morning."[1]

Yasutaro died on April 3, 1869. Jinzaburo tells us that Yasutaro was happy and at peace, thanks to Mary's comforting and tender presence. She brought peace to Yasutaro those cold nights in the deep snow. And she will bring peace this Christmas, and every Christmas, for all who seek the *Prince of Peace*.

FOUR

BEHOLD CHRIST OUR JOY

THIRD SUNDAY OF ADVENT

PREPARE THE WAY

Our lectio for the third Sunday of Advent—Gaudete Sunday—brings us into the home of Mary and Joseph in Nazareth. There was no greater joy to the families of Israel than the arrival of a new baby! We encounter Mary and Joseph in a busy but joyful moment of preparing for Christ's birth. Together, Mary and Joseph make a gift for the Christ Child, and all the while they work, their *hearts cry out with joy and gladness: for among [them] is the great and Holy One of Israel.*

Fittingly, the joy of the third Sunday of Advent is amplified in various traditions that prepare our own homes for the baby Jesus. In Rome, for example, the pope blesses all the *bambinelli,* or figures of the baby Jesus, which the faithful will place in their own manger scenes on Christmas morning. Through such traditional observations of Advent, the joy of Christmas Day grows even more palpable to our hands and our hearts.

Reflecting these hands-on preparations, the fourth lectio of our Marian journey imagines Mary's joy by focusing our attention on one of the psalms for the Third Sunday of Advent. Interestingly, this "responsorial psalm" is not a psalm at all, but a passage from Isaiah, our faithful prophet of Advent! Meditating on this scriptural text joins our joy to Mary's joy (and to Joseph's!) as we prepare to behold the Christ Child in our own homes on Christmas morning. With the first reading at Mass, we listen. But, when we participate in the responsorial psalm at Mass, *we sing*! Indeed, singing the responsorial psalms of Advent, *we respond* with heart and voice to the good news that is unfolding before our eyes, week to week. As we enter the third week of Advent, may our journey be fired by the joy and gladness of Christmas drawing near. Let us *rejoice and exult with all [our] heart!*

BEHOLD THE WORD

ZEPHANIAH 3:14–18

Sing aloud, O daughter of Zion;
shout, O Israel!
Rejoice and exult with all your heart,
O daughter of Jerusalem!
. . . The King of Israel, the LORD, is in your midst;
. . . Do not fear, O Zion;
let not your hands grow weak.
The LORD, your God, is in your midst,

. . . he will rejoice over you with gladness,
he will renew you in his love;
he will exult over you with loud singing
as on a day of festival.

ISAIAH 12:2–6

"Behold, God is my salvation;
I will trust, and will not be afraid;
for the LORD God is my strength and my song,
and he has become my salvation."
With joy you will draw water from the wells of salvation. And you will say in that day:
"Give thanks to the LORD,
call upon his name;
make known his deeds among the nations,
proclaim that his name is exalted.
"Sing praises to the LORD, for he has done gloriously;
let this be known in all the earth.
Shout, and sing with joy, O inhabitant of Zion,
for great in your midst is the Holy One of Israel!

CONSIDER THE SCENE

In this lectio, Mary and Joseph join us in the psalms we sing on Gaudete Sunday. Like us, they repeatedly echo the response from Isaiah: "Sing praises to the LORD, for he has done gloriously. . . . Shout, and sing for joy . . . for great in your midst is the Holy One of Israel" (12:5–6). In this choir of responses, the joy elicited by God's presence resounds across the ages, from Isaiah's crying out and Zephaniah's exhortation to "sing . . . shout . . . rejoice," to Mary and Joseph's exulting hearts, and finally to our glad chorus of rejoicing. Why? Because Christ will be here soon. Very soon!

Again, like us, Mary and Joseph have made many preparations for Christ's birth, some very practical, and others less so! In the moment imagined by this lectio, we pause with them as they, in their enduring gladness, make some less-practical preparations: a gift for the Holy One already present in their home. They desire to work on this gift for the Christ Child more than any other task at hand, even those tasks necessary for their long journey to Bethlehem. Their gift is a sign of gratitude. Their handiwork is a generous, almost extravagant, moment of doting on the unborn Babe. With humility, they revel in the fact of God made man . . . made a baby boy . . . and in their home! It is certainly a delight for us to join them!

ISAIAH'S IMAGERY AND MARY'S EMBROIDERY

It is delightful to see the joy spoken of by Isaiah come to its full fruition. In his own time, Isaiah's thematic imagery of new growth conveyed the joy Israel felt as they were liberated from their exile in Babylon, where Israel was held captive for nearly fifty years. Isaiah describes Israel's jubilation in images of a once barren land being refreshed and reblooming with new life. Here are two of the more beautiful passages the lectio draws upon:

> *The wilderness and the dry land shall be glad,*
> *the desert shall rejoice and blossom;*
> *like the lily it shall blossom abundantly,*
> *and rejoice with joy and singing . . .*

> *For waters shall break forth in the wilderness,*
> *and streams in the desert . . .* (Is 35:1–2, 6)
>
> *. . . as the earth brings forth its shoots,*
> *and as a garden causes what is sown in it to spring up,*
> *so the Lord God will cause righteousness and praise*
> *to spring forth before all the nations.* (Is 61:11)

What depths of joy arise from Isaiah's poignant imagery! Today, we understand Isaiah's barren land to be the soul bereft of God's presence through sin. But now, at Christmas, the soul will rebloom, "watered" again by God's presence.

In our lectio, Mary, quite literally, takes Isaiah's imagery into her hands as she creates her gift for the Christ Child. We imagine her sewing a flowered field for Joseph's wooden sheep to graze and play in. The embroidered field is a garden composed of Isaiah's streams, lilies, and grasses.

THE GOOD SHEPHERD

Thus, as we bring Mary's meadow and Joseph's wooden sheep together, we can also imagine Christ as the Good Shepherd (see John 10:7–16), ourselves as sheep, and the re-blossomed land as our home, where, Christ, the great and *Holy One of Israel*, is in our midst. Our response? A Marian cry: *I will greatly rejoice in the LORD; my soul shall exult in my God* (Is 61:10).

JOSEPH'S SILENT JOY

While Mary sews, Joseph, the just man, the carpenter, the husband of Mary, quietly carves toy sheep. The silence of Mary and Joseph's home compliments the singing of their hearts.

We can see ourselves in their home, between them, smiling and working!

In this silence is an expectation of a child, yes! But this child is the Word made flesh, the Holy One who will soon speak to us in a child's voice. Joseph joins Mary in this expectant silence, their hearts clamoring with shouts of joy from within their chests. Together, they await the sound of Christ's voice, the laughter of his play, and the blossoming of his presence in their home.

THE CROSS ON GAUDETE SUNDAY?

But, wait, there is one last note. We must place our joy firmly in the fullness of God's saving love. The opening of our lectio fills us with the scent of freshly cut wood. Naturally, this is first and foremost a reference to Joseph's work as a carpenter and his generous preparations for the coming child. But the scents of wood not only also point us toward Christ's crib—a sheep's manger—but to Christ's Cross. Together, these capture the fullness of God's redemptive love. Christ's whole life, from crib to Cross, is lived for us. Take in the scents of cedar and pine, cypress and olive wood; breathe in the aroma of Christ's love, for as Tradition tells us, these were the four kinds of wood used for his Cross. The love that begins to be heralded on Christmas morning is an "I love you" spoken by every moment of Christ's whole life.

PRAY WITH LECTIO DIVINA

The scent of freshly cut wood filled the house. As Mary passes through Joseph's woodshop, she smells the scraps of cedar, pine, and cypress that lay at Joseph's feet. In his hand, a small wooden lamb is slowly emerging from a piece of olive wood. On his work bench stand three more small objects: two sheep, with their wool finely carved into curls, and their plain pine box manger. Soon the small wooden lamb, to be made just the right size for a child's hand, would complete the set.

Mary worked quietly, too; many brightly colored threads were strung across her lap. Her heart, however, sang and shouted in her chest: "Sing for joy . . . great in [our] midst is the Holy One of Israel!" Her joy overflowed and filled the silent house, animating her final preparations, together with Joseph—a gift for the Holy One.

In Mary's hands, a few scraps of old cloak were being made new by her handiwork: lilies threaded into bloom, green grasses sprouted up, and blue stitches became tiny streams (see Isaiah 35:1–2, 6). These bits of embroidered garden transformed a brown and barren reed basket into the fields of Nazareth, perfect for a little shepherd boy and his hand-carved, curly-haired sheep (see John 10:7–16).

This gift was a work of love, shared by Mary and Joseph. In these last quiet but glad-filled days of expectation, Mary and Joseph thought of nothing but the baby, the very joy of their home.

Of course, they knew there were more mundane preparations to make, especially since word had arrived of the imminent Roman census. Mary and Joseph would have to journey to Bethlehem to be enrolled. As her day of delivery was near, Mary knew the journey would not be easy. Yet the angel Gabriel had said, "be not afraid," Mary. "Rejoice!" And so, she did, and Joseph with her.

With every stitch, Mary's heart continually sang out with joy and thanksgiving: "Among us is the great and Holy One of Israel! He is here in our home, within my flesh, pressed up against my happy heart." The things of the world could not distract her joy. The words of Isaiah, so familiar to her of late, filled her mind:

> *Behold, God is my salvation;*
> *I will trust, and will not be afraid;*
> *for the* LORD *God is my strength and my song,*
> *and he has become my salvation."*
> *With joy [I have drawn] water from the wells of salvation,*
> *[flowing like light through my soul].*

As Mary's heart sang such praises to the Lord, Joseph silently placed the olive wood lamb in the reed basket. His own heart was shouting with exultation and singing to the Lord with joy.

CONTEMPLATE WITH VISIO DIVINA

Gaze at this painting for a few minutes. What things catch your attention? What do you notice first, and why? Take in every detail—the colors, light, depiction of the created world. What emotions and insights well up in you?

FOLLOW MARY TODAY

> *"Hail, O Lady, Holy Queen, God's Holy Mother Mary!*
> *You have been made the Virgin Church*
> *and chosen by the most Holy Father in heaven . . .*
> *Hail his Palace! Hail his Tabernacle! Hail his Dwelling Place!*
> *Hail his Garment! Hail his Handmaid! Hail his Mother!"*[1]

This is one of St. Francis of Assisi's many prayers, or "salutations," for the Blessed Virgin Mary. This saint's devotion to Mary is often overshadowed by his admiration for creation and for the humanity of Christ, which had its beginning in the Incarnation and in Mary. As we can see through his prayer, St. Francis indeed had a deep devotion to Our Lady, God's holy Mother Mary.

Francis of Assisi is famous for creating the first manger scene. The first manger brought Francis so much joy that he wept at the sight of the baby Jesus upon the hay. Today we continue to imitate St. Francis and share his joy when we set up manger scenes in our homes, setting our *bambinelli*—figures of the baby Jesus that are sometimes blessed at Church—amidst the hay.

As the story goes, St. Francis spent Christmas in Greccio, Italy, in 1223. Greccio is not so far from Assisi, but it would have been quite a trek on foot! Greccio is a hill town and has many craggy cave-like spaces, even in the center of town. It was one of these caves that reminded Francis of Christ's cave-like stable in Bethlehem and led him to ask that it be filled with hay and even a few farm animals so as to recreate the scene of Christ's Nativity. That year in Greccio, for the first time ever, Christmas Mass was celebrated in a craggy cave amidst a living Christmas

Creche! In his 2019 apostolic letter *Admirabile Signum* (Wondrous Sign!), on the meaning and importance of the Nativity scene, Pope Francis speaks of this awesome tradition, begun by St. Francis and still practiced today in our parishes and homes:

> With what emotion should we arrange the mountains, streams, sheep and shepherds in the nativity scene! As we do so, we are reminded that, as the prophets had foretold, all creation rejoices in the coming of the Messiah . . . When, at Christmas, we place the statue of the Infant Jesus in the manger, the nativity scene suddenly comes alive. God appears as a child, for us to take into our arms. . . . and in this way, he wished to reveal the greatness of his love.[2]

The tradition of the nativity scene, first imagined by St. Francis, is a joy-filled Marian ritual that can reveal the greatness of God's love within our own homes. Pope Francis tells us, "The nativity scene is like a living Gospel rising up from the pages of sacred Scripture."[3] It was Francis's joy to make the Gospel visible for all to behold. All who prepare a nativity scene in their homes bring the Gospel to life. This is a very Mary-like activity and gift of love.

FIVE

BEHOLD CHRIST OUR LOVE

FOURTH SUNDAY OF ADVENT

PREPARE THE WAY

The Fourth Sunday of Advent has arrived! All of Israel has been called to return to their own cities by Augustus Caesar. There, all were to be enrolled during the first census. Accordingly, this lectio prepares us to set off on one more journey with Mary and Joseph—to Bethlehem, the "home" of their ancestor, David.

Mary's journey with Joseph, from their home in Nazareth to the "house of David," parallels a spiritual journey unfolding in Mary's mind and heart. On her journey between sand and star, she contemplates God's question to her ancestor, David: *Would you build me a house to live in?*

It is a marvelous question! One we should all ask ourselves. This week, we ask it with Mary. The question suggests a God who desires to be with us, to have a "home" amongst us. To love us!

The suggestion of such a love becomes a joyful truth to Mary (and to us!) as her two journeys intertwine. As Mary travels through the cosmic beauty of creation, she also journeys toward a greater understanding of her own flesh as God's "house." Amidst the expanse of winter in the Judean desert, and with the cosmic child yet wrapped in her womb, Mary encounters God's love for us as a dazzling desire to enter our hearts as into a home.

Thus, Mary's contemplation of God's "house" illuminates this week's Advent theme of love. As we turn our faces toward Bethlehem, Mary prepares us to encounter both the stunning "house" of creation and the attention God lavishes on the human heart as he seeks his entrance there.

Perhaps we can even remember Mary's experience whenever we prepare to receive the Eucharist this final week of Advent: "Lord I am not worthy that you should enter under my roof, but only say the word and my soul shall be healed!"

BEHOLD THE WORD

ISAIAH 7:10–14

Again the Lord *spoke to A'haz, "Ask a sign of the* Lord *your God; let it be deep as Sheol or high as heaven." But A'haz said, "I will not ask, and I will not put the* Lord *to the test." And [Isaiah] said, "Hear then, O house of David! Is it too little for you to weary men, that you weary my God also? Therefore the Lord himself will give you a sign. Behold, a virgin shall conceive and bear a son, and shall call his name Imman'u-el.*

MICAH 5:2–4

You, O Bethlehem of Eph'rathah,
who are little to be among the clans of Judah,
from you shall come forth for me
one who is to be ruler in Israel,
whose origin is from of old,
from ancient days.
Therefore he shall give them up until the time
when she who has labor pains has brought forth;
then the rest of his brethren shall return
to the sons of Israel.
And he shall stand and feed his flock in the strength
of the LORD,
in the majesty of the name of the LORD his God.
And they dwell secure, for now he shall be great
to the ends of the earth.

2 SAMUEL 7:1–5, 8–12, 14, 16

Now when the king dwelt in his house, and the LORD had given him rest from all his enemies round about, the king said to Nathan the prophet, "See now, I dwell in a house of cedar, but the ark of God dwells in a tent." And Nathan said to the king, "Go, do all that you have in your heart; for the LORD is with you."

But that same night the word of the LORD came to Nathan: "Go and tell my servant David, 'Thus says the LORD: Would you build me a house to dwell in? . . . Now therefore thus you shall say to my servant David, "Thus says the LORD of hosts, I took you from the pasture, from following the sheep, that you should be prince over my people Israel; and have been with you wherever you went, and have cut off all your enemies from before you; and I will make for you a great name, like the name of the great ones of the earth. And I will appoint a place for my people Israel, and will plant them, that they may dwell in their own place, and be disturbed no more; and violent men shall afflict them no more, as formerly, from the time that I appointed judges over my people Israel; and I will give you rest from all your enemies. Moreover the LORD declares to you that the LORD will make you a house. When your days are fulfilled and you lie down with your fathers, I will raise up your offspring after you, who shall come forth from your body, and I will establish his kingdom. . . . I will be his father, and he shall be my son. . . . Your house and your kingdom shall be made sure forever before me; your throne shall be established forever.'"

CONSIDER THE SCENE

Could we ever behold a night sky like those Mary and Joseph experienced? Today, man-made light dims the majesty of the night sky in so many places. We can only imagine the magnificence beheld by Mary and Joseph!

THE NIGHT SKY

Scripture helps us imagine a truly dark and star-studded night sky. In Genesis, for example, God calls the sun, moon, and stars to shine forth from the midst of the black darkness called "Night" (see Genesis 1:3–8). Marveling at the majesty of such a sight, the psalmist voices all that we might feel, too: *When I look at your heavens, the work of your fingers, the moon and the stars which you have established; what is man that you are mindful of him, and the son of man that you care for him?* (Ps 8:3–4).

With the help of these poetic lines from scripture, a gorgeous winter night surrounds us and dazzles us. It is this winter sky, full of stars, meteors, and planets, that is the backdrop for our Marian lectio on love.

Under this sky, and with Mary at our side, its natural beauty not only awes us, but it also silently speaks to us of God, our one and only Creator, and all his cosmic works of creation, including ourselves. We may feel small beneath the night sky, but that is all the more reason it helps us to know that God loves us.

With Mary, we can even befriend these stars! Scripture frequently personifies them. Mary was likely familiar with their happy rejoicing, as in Job or Baruch. There, the stars laugh and sing, delighted to be God's creatures. With Mary during Advent, we might hear the stars' song as the sort of rejoicing appropriate to the approach of Christmas Day. Besides, we know that a particular star will soon shine out to announce the birth of our Lord to all the world.

GOD'S HOUSEHOLD

As we befriend the stars with Mary, they begin to tell us also about the extent of God's household. Through the Incarnation, God comes to dwell within his household in a new way. Before the Incarnation, before Mary's yes, God had still dwelt with Israel *on each stage of their journey* (see Exodus 40:38), but in fire and cloud, in tent, tabernacle, and temple. But now, with Mary's help, the stars tell us that she is God's tent-tabernacle. From her flesh, God's love will flame out and make his home among us.

The cosmic Creator is the lover of our souls. He is both God and a cosmic child—a babe in Mary's womb. Thus, we are nestled with Mary in the contrast between the household of her flesh and the household that is the whole of creation.

PERSONAL PARTICULARS

Christmas emphasizes the particular: the God who is the lover of each and every soul. We encounter this love in the concreteness of the home of Mary and Joseph in Nazareth, the smallness of Bethlehem, and the counting of every family and every family member in Caesar's census.

Thus, in this lectio, we have placed ourselves alongside Mary as she observes the contrast of sky and flesh, of cosmic and minute realities. We have journeyed with Mary as she comes to understand God's house. Just as the night sky expands above her, as the sands of the desert go out before her, and as a profound awareness of God's love anchors itself within her, we, too, are surrounded by God's love. With Mary, we become aware that God wishes to be born in the flesh-and-blood particularity of our own hearts, each and every one.

PRAY WITH LECTIO DIVINA

The morning was still dark when Mary heard Joseph drawing cold water from the garden well. It was time to get up, to gather their last few things, and to go. The Emperor, Augustus Caesar, had called everyone to return to the place of their birth in order to be counted. All the families of Israel were returning to the places they first called "home" in the Promised Land. Mary and

Joseph were traveling to Bethlehem, "the city of David," for they were of the *house and lineage of David*.

Upon her bed that night (see Song of Solomon 3:1), Mary had lain awake, pondering the words that God had posed to David: "Would you build me a house to live in?" It was a curious question: a house for God! A place to dwell with him! And even more curious: He desires it! These thoughts had gripped Mary's heart. She turned them over and over in her mind.

Still lost in contemplation, Mary wrapped herself snuggly in her sapphire blue traveling cloak. But for Joseph, a small grey donkey, and the stone well, the garden was empty. No flowers appeared there yet (see Song of Solomon 2:12), for winter still lingered in Israel, when the barren desert magnifies the starry sky as a dazzling and breathtaking expanse. On their way to be counted and "enrolled," Mary and Joseph would travel under a firmament of countless stars!

The desert expanse seemed to speak with God's voice: *The Lord declares to you that the Lord will make you a house.* A long journey stretched before Mary and Joseph up and over the steep and rocky hills that crisscross the Judean desert, then up higher still and further over through the shepherds' fields toward Bethlehem, small and insignificant against the horizon.

Mary thought: "Your house and your kingdom are firm forever before me." And she contemplated this "house" of the Lord spread all around her: rock and hill, desert sky, sand and starlight. God had called forth the dry land, and set each and every star in its place (see Genesis 1:10, 14–15). This was God's house! And still, God's question came to her: "Would you build me a house to live in?"

With her face to the desert sky, Mary's thoughts turned to Job. God had questioned him, too, and that question now seemed to echo off the cold desert rocks: *Where were you when I laid the foundation of the earth? . . . when the morning stars sang together, and all the sons of God shouted for joy?* (Jb 38:4, 7).

The Lord declares to you that the Lord will make you a house. And you have, Lord! You have made us a house, of sand and light. It goes forever before us and it expands all around us in land and sky. And yet, you ask me for *a house to live in*? Are you not here in the expanse of sand and light? Are you not here in the words turning in my thoughts and in my heart?

Looking about her, Mary was overcome with a sudden understanding of just how well God loved her. He loved her well enough to ask her for a house. Yes! God loved her well enough to ask her *to be his house*! Ah! Mary turned God's words over again in her mind: "Your house and your kingdom shall be made sure forever [within] me!"

Listen, O house of David! The universe is vast, *[God's] greatness [reaches] to the ends of the earth*! Yet, today, a star-song of cosmic glory sings to us from a new house, "built" by David: *The Lord himself [has given us a] sign: a virgin [has conceived], and [will] bear a son, and shall call his name Imman'u-el.*

Amidst the vast landscape of sand and stars, God chose Mary as his humble house of flesh, wrapped now in a blue traveling cloak and settled upon a small grey donkey. The singular Christ, that cosmic child, was placed in *her* care. Today she would carry Immanuel to Bethlehem, "the city of David," and there, under the same infinity of stars, divine love woven and wed within her womb would come to dwell among all people for the *Lord will make [of] you a house!*

CONTEMPLATE WITH VISIO DIVINA

Gaze at this painting for a few minutes. What things catch your attention? What do you notice first, and why? Take in every detail—the colors, light, depiction of the created world. What emotions and insights well up in you?

FOLLOW MARY TODAY

"I will be love." These are the ecstatic words of St. Thérèse of Lisieux declaring her vocation. She wrote them into the story of her soul near the end of her short life. Yet, her sense of her purpose began to develop within her at a very young age, as she encountered the beauty of God's creation and the tender motherhood of the Virgin Mary.

As a child, great fields of wildflowers, "starred with poppies, cornflowers and daises" moved Thérèse's heart with profound emotion.[1] So did the sea: Its "majestic roaring" waves filled her "with a sense of the power and majesty of God."[2] She loved "far distances, wide-open spaces, and . . . great trees."[3]

Thérèse tells us that one evening, as she walked home with her father and her sisters, she "gazed with delight at the stars shining above. There was one group in particular which filled [her] with joy, for [she] noticed that it was in the shape of the letter T[:] 'I pointed it out to Daddy and told him that my name was written in heaven . . . without looking where I was going, I kept my face turned up to the sky.'"[4]

Included in her awe for creation was Thérèse's intimate sense of God's love *for her*. Once, when she was ill, this intimate love came through the statue of the Blessed Virgin in Thérèse's bedroom, while she lay sick in bed. As her sisters prayed for her to the Blessed Virgin, the statue "glowed with a beauty beyond anything [Thérèse] had ever seen. Her face was alive with kindness and an infinite tenderness, but it was her enchanting smile which really moved [Thérèse] to the depths."[5]

The beauty of creation and the beauty of Christ's mother both moved Thérèse to love God profoundly. Through both, one in its vast and moving majesty, the other in its intimate and personal particularity, Thérèse received God's love. As she writes in the *Story of a Soul*, "The sun shines equally both on tall cedars and on every tiny flower. In just the same way God looks after every soul as if it had no equal."[6]

These last days of Advent invite us to approach Christmas Day, not only with Mary, but with Thérèse, too, contemplating creation's awesome array of signs pointing to God's love. God's cosmic and creative love will soon be witnessed in the singular and intimate revelation of Mary's son. Christ asks to be born in your own heart, and St. Thérèse can help you embrace him there: *I will be love*.

SIX

BEHOLD THE HOLY BIRTH

CHRISTMAS DAY

PREPARE THE WAY

Christmas is unlike any other time of the year. Christmas Eve is filled with a calm excitement, and Christmas morning is all awe and joy. As we welcome the Christ Child, the things of everyday life swell with sacred significance: bright night skies, warm fires, the scents of the holiday kitchen, the faces of family and friends.

For several weeks now, we have journeyed toward this wonderful day with Mary. She has helped us prepare our homes for her son, and to enlarge our hearts to welcome the boundless love of God. And now, on this day of all days, we behold the simple reality of a baby. And yet, in beholding this newborn babe, the eyes of faith behold our Lord and God.

We never tire of this awesome beholding. We never tire of drawing near to Mary and her child. Our hearts desire Christmas Day every day. Let us see your love always, Lord! Let the revelation of this divine child spill beyond Christmas and illuminate all our days!

Over the many years since the first Christmas night, human hands have worked to depict the sacred love revealed at Christmas. We place these images in our churches, our homes, and our hearts—the craggy tomb-like scene of ancient icons; the luminous baby Jesus of richly-hued oil paintings; the ox and ass peering into their manger at the human infant; fine figurines painstakingly carved of stone and wood; even the glowing, plastic figures on many a front lawn.

In this lectio, we imagine the humble night on which Christ was born. And we seek, with Mary, our heart's greatest desire: to behold God's awesome love for us in the countenance of her son. Our long journey has been well worth it! Let's do some wondrous beholding.

BEHOLD THE WORD

LUKE 2:1–21

In those days a decree went out from Caesar Augustus that all the world should be enrolled. This was the first enrollment, when Quirin'ius was governor of Syria. And all went to be enrolled, each to his own city. And Joseph also went up from Galilee, from the city of Nazareth, to Judea, to the city of David, which is called Bethlehem, because he was of the house and lineage of David, to be enrolled with Mary, his betrothed, who was with child. And while they were there, the time came for her to be delivered. And she gave birth to her first-born son and wrapped him in swaddling cloths, and laid him in a manger, because there was no place for them in the inn. And in that region there were shepherds out in the field, keeping watch over their flock by night. And an angel of the Lord appeared to them, and the glory of the Lord shone around them, and they were filled with fear. And the angel said to them, "Be not afraid; for behold, I bring you good news of a great joy which will come to all the people; for to you is born this day in the city of David a Savior, who is Christ the Lord. And this will be a sign for you: you will find a baby wrapped in swaddling cloths and lying in a manger." And suddenly there was with the angel a multitude of the heavenly host praising God and saying,

> *"Glory to God in the highest,*
> *and on earth peace among men with whom he is pleased!"*

When the angels went away from them into heaven, the shepherds said to one another, "Let us go over to Bethlehem and see this thing that has happened, which the Lord has made known to us." And they went with haste, and found Mary and Joseph, and the baby lying in a manger. And when they saw it they made known the saying which had been told them concerning this child; and all who heard it wondered at what the shepherds told them. But Mary kept all these things, pondering them in her heart. And the shepherds returned, glorifying and praising God for all they had heard and seen, as it had been told them.

CONSIDER THE SCENE

Our lectio begins in a far-off place: the little town of Bethlehem and the shepherds' fields that surround it. Yet, even though our lectio unfolds far from our own homes, the opening scene remains familiar. We imagine families and friends gathered at the table and talking of the journeys that brought them together. All are happy, though they know not yet the real reason for such a happy night, or for what reason providence, God's loving care, brought them to be together this night.

CHRIST'S BIRTH AND GENESIS

As scripture tells us, the little town of Bethlehem is bustling and filled to overflowing. There is no room for Mary and Joseph at the inn. They settle for a lowly stable, still in use. As we conjure the hidden scene of Christ's birth, elements of the creation story weave in, reminding us just who is born in this unexpected place. The Light of the World. The Light of Love itself. *Let there be light!*

MOTHER AND CHILD

Another familiar scene follows: a mother adoring her newborn child. We behold the one who *is* love with Mary. We see her wrap and swaddle him. We imagine her longing to hold him as he sleeps peacefully on the hay. We see her take him into her arms and lay her face upon his, wholly rapt in his presence and desirous of a kiss.

Thus, while we don't venture a description of the Christ Child's face, we dwell on the touch of a baby's sweetly soft skin. We are led into Mary's beholding through our own memories of similar experiences: the singular feeling of an infant's delectably round cheeks under one's lips. Every kiss is an experience of pure joy! And, here, we get to go one step further: The baby's kissable skin announces the happy reality of the Incarnation.

KISSES

Alongside the kissable reality of the infant Jesus, the Incarnation itself has been described as a "kiss" across the Christian Tradition.

In a commentary on the Song of Solomon, by a twelfth-century monk named Honorius, the kiss of the Song's opening verse ("Let him kiss me with the kisses of his mouth!") is the kiss that Mary gives to her son and that she receives from the baby Jesus. But for many centuries before Honorius, Christians read the Song of Solomon as the best text of all texts for expressing the heights of our loving rapture when speaking with God in prayer. Indeed, our Tradition tells us that God himself gave us this language so that we could speak of such experiences of love!

Building on these traditions of interpretation, we extend the language of the Song of Solomon to Mary's love for her son, and to Joseph's love for them both.

THE SHEPHERD'S BEHOLDING

Mary and Joseph's beholding of the wonder before them is only broken by the sudden and melodious song of angels and shepherds, the latter come to see the sign announced to them by the angels:

> "Be not afraid; for behold, I bring you good news of a great joy which will come to all the people; for to you is born this day in the city of David a Savior, who is Christ the Lord. And this will be a sign for you: you will find a baby wrapped in swaddling cloths and lying in a manger." (Lk 2:10–12)

Often, the scene of the shepherds and angels is one of our central foci on Christmas, all the "scenes" of the Nativity story folding in upon one another. But here we experience the arrival of the shepherds as a "sudden" interruption of the most central event: gazing upon the Christ Child. Like us, the shepherds have come to find the child of whom the angels (and all the scriptures!) have spoken. They arrive and join us in our gazing, filled with exceeding joy.

Together we behold this child in the arms of his mother, calm and happy. All is good. Indeed, all is very good.

PRAY WITH LECTIO DIVINA

The stone-hewn homes of Bethlehem were aglow with firelight. There, families and travelers shared their bread and told stories, new and old. Beyond their glowing windows, still more travelers crowded the market squares and overflowed down the streets. Bethlehem, *little* and *small*, bustling and bursting, could not welcome a single traveler more—not even if that traveler was "of the royal house of David"; not even if that traveler was the tiniest of all travelers: a small child ready to be born that night.

Day and night, the *shepherds in the fields* had been keeping vigil over a procession of endless travelers crossing their fields. They came from all directions, emerging from the desert horizon, moving through sheep-filled pastures, and disappearing into Bethlehem, stone-grey and waiting. Tonight, however, the fields were left again to the shepherds and their flocks. All was calm. All was good.

Bustling Bethlehem had also grown calm. The weary travelers slept soundly, tucked into every and any corner they could lay their heads. All, that is, but one pair of travelers: Mary and Joseph.

They had arrived in Bethlehem with the day's last light; a single star appearing in the night sky. Mary, whose "time had come," was full as the fullest moon, still wrapped in the deep blue of night. Again and again they were told, "We have no room!" There was not a single room for them in the whole city of David!

Instead of a guest room, Mary and Joseph were welcomed into the stony corner of a stable, still occupied by an ox, an ass, and several curly-haired sheep. Hay was strewn across the floor, still smelling sweetly like grass. The glittering night sky peaked around wind-worn stones and through crooked cracks, as if to whisper God's command upon the hidden scene, *Let there be light*!

Thus, it was there, in a stable, the home of sheep and cows, that *[Mary] gave birth to her first-born son and wrapped him in swaddling cloths, and laid him in a manger*. Mary's heart exulted as never before, simply to behold him asleep on the hay, luminous.

> "Ah, you are beautiful, my love, my [son] . . . truly lovely (Song of Solomon 1:15–16 NRSVCE). Let me rock you in my arms and upon my knees. O, [let me] kiss [you] with the kisses of [my] mouth!" (Sg 1:2)

With unsurpassed tenderness, the new mother picked up her son and held him close, wrapping him in the folds of her cloak. His skin was soft against her cheeks and kissable under her lips.

Happy in this hidden, humble scene, Joseph gazed upon Mary and child. He, too, was enraptured with the child, but even more so to behold them together. Mary's whole countenance was flushed with affection, pure and loving. *Who is this that looks forth like the dawn, fair as the moon, bright as the sun?* (Sg 6:10).

And then suddenly, in a single moment, Mary and Joseph were drawn out of their rapturous gazing. They were no longer alone. Singing echoed through the cave, merry and bright!

Mary immediately recognized the sweet, melodious voice of angels. But who was their rich and sonorous accompaniment? Together, the voices were singing a hymn never before heard:

> "Glory to God in the highest,
> and on earth peace among men with whom he is pleased!" (Lk 2:14)

Shepherds, fresh from the fields, and afire with awe, came softly into the cave, still hymning, low and sweet. There, in Mary's arms, they beheld the *Good News of great joy for all* with exceeding wonder: Swaddled and draped in blue, a glorious babe lay sleeping.

CONTEMPLATE WITH VISIO DIVINA

Gaze at this painting for a few minutes. What things catch your attention? What do you notice first, and why? Take in every detail—the colors, light, depiction of the created world. What emotions and insights well up in you?

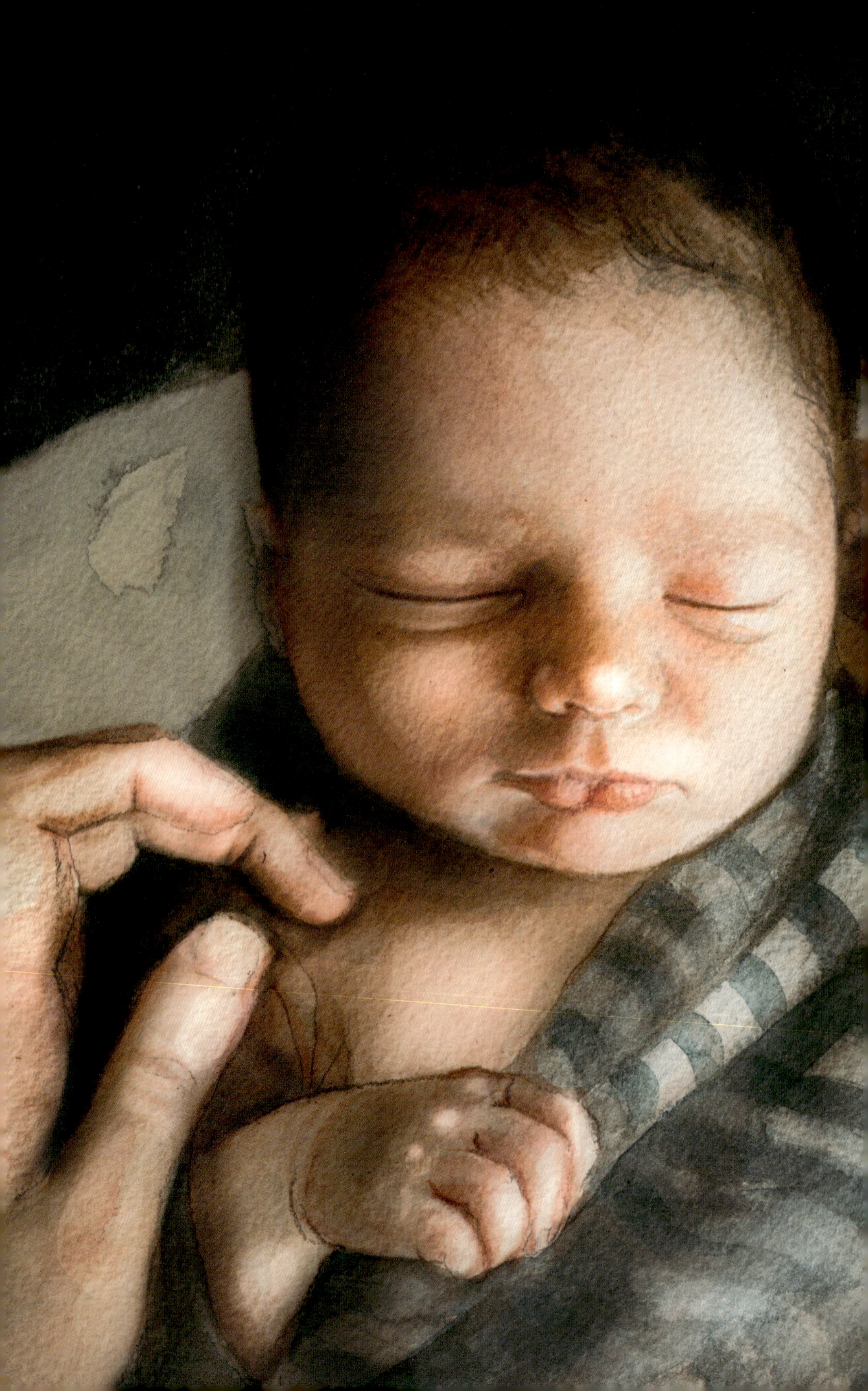

FOLLOW MARY TODAY

Because St. Joseph was Mary's husband, we can imagine his regard for his beautiful wife on Christmas Day. Mary's beauty was surely magnified by her humility and charity. But on Christmas Day, she is also simply aglow with the reality of being a new mother, and finally beholding her firstborn son. Thus, in our lectio just now, we imagined Joseph gazing upon Mary as a new mother, *fair as the moon* and ravishing *like the dawn.*

Scripture tells us very little about St. Joseph. Indeed, we are privy to none of the details of his life, or that of the Holy Family, and Joseph himself doesn't say a single word. Still, scripture invites us to imagine Joseph's love not only for Mary, but for the Christ Child, too. Joseph quietly guarded Jesus from the moment of his birth, and protected him as he grew.

Joseph's loving protection ensured that *Jesus increased in wisdom and in stature, and in favor with God and man* (Lk 2:52). As an innocent babe, born on Christmas Night, Jesus was small and helpless, dependent on Mary and Joseph to mother and father the Good News, the Gospel himself, into the world. King Herod, for one, hoped to kill the Christ Child. And he could have except that Joseph, in his selfless love for Mary and Jesus, protected them both from such evils, for Christ's *hour* had not yet come.

Like St. Joseph, we, too, can gaze upon the wondrous dawning of the Gospel into our world. From St. Joseph, we can learn to welcome the Christ Child into our own lives and to guard and protect the Gospel, "mothering" and "fathering" Christ into the world. With St. Joseph, we can cradle and nourish the Gospel in our hearts, until someday, perhaps silently, the Christ Child will be discovered and beheld there by another, like some unexpected holy gift, *fair as the moon, bright as the sun.*

SEVEN

BEHOLD OUR MOTHER

SOLEMNITY OF MARY, THE HOLY MOTHER OF GOD

PREPARE THE WAY

On the Octave of Christmas, we celebrate the Solemnity of Mary, the Holy Mother of God. In some ways, this feast is like a second annunciation, for it is the day on which we celebrate the naming of the Christ Child according to the name announced by the angel Gabriel: "Jesus." To this joy, we add the title of Mary as "Mother of God." In naming her son, Mary names herself "Mother."

Thus, to reflect on the intimate moment in which Jesus is named is to reflect upon Mary's divine motherhood. Beholding

Mary in this moment of naming is to gaze upon her own self-realization of her divine motherhood. This is her son, "Jesus," and she is his mother, the Theotokos, the God-bearer or Mother of God!

As we enter into this scene with Mary, we encounter all that Mary has been pondering since the annunciation. Much has been said to her—by the angel, by Elizabeth, by the shepherds, and by God through scripture—and it all converges in this moment in two words: "Jesus" and "Mama." May we dwell with Mary this week and gaze upon motherhood itself, tender and joyful.

BEHOLD THE WORD

NUMBERS 6:24–26

The LORD bless you and keep you:
The LORD make his face to shine upon you, and be
gracious to you:
The LORD lift up his countenance upon you, and
give you peace.

PSALM 67:1–2

[R. May God bless us in his mercy.]
May God be gracious to us and bless us
and make his face to shine upon us,
that your way may be known upon earth,
your saving power among all nations.

LUKE 2:19

> *Mary kept all these things,*
> *pondering them in her heart.*

LUKE 2:21

And at the end of eight days, when he was circumcised, he was called Jesus, the name given by the angel before he was conceived in the womb.

CONSIDER THE SCENE

It is an ancient Jewish custom to name your son on the eighth day after his birth. Here Mary and Joseph follow this custom, naming Jesus in the stable cave at Bethlehem, *at the end of eight days*. For any of us who have named a child, we know the significance of this moment: It weaves a web of relationship between parent and child, the two beholding each other in love.

NAMING NAMES

A child's name is a special significance within ancient Judaism, where names carry a prophetic quality. The name "Jesus" was given by the angel Gabriel and means "God saves." As we know, and as we have been celebrating these eight days, Jesus is Immanuel, "God with us."

The act of naming a child in Judaism also has special significance for the mother. In her act of naming her child, she is also defined as mother. Thus, we have the beautiful coincidence of contemplating Mary as "Mother of God" in the same moment that she names her son, "Jesus."

RETURNING TO THE ANNUNCIATION

Playing on this double act of naming, our lectio returns to the imagery of the lectio with which we began our Marian journey: the annunciation. There, we imagined a garden scene, in which the angel Gabriel came to Mary at her well, where she was drawing water. There, the angel named Mary, full of grace. We pictured this full of grace-ness as water and light flowing through Mary's whole being.

Mary again feels this flow of grace as she names Jesus, who, as an infant, and in an echo of Isaiah (*a shoot shall sprout* . . .), is fertile soil and a blossoming shoot. But these images of water, light, and soil are also complementary images; they belong together. Water and light nurture the life of a plant, rooted in the soil.

In our lectio, when speaking of Mary and Jesus, the nurturing happens not only from mother to son, but also from son to mother. Mary mothers Jesus's humanity; Jesus mothers Mary's grace. She waters him with her milk; he nurtures her with the light of love. And so, he blossoms as her son, and she blossoms as his mother. Dante once put it this way: Mary, that Mystical Rose, is the singular Mother of God who is yet "the daughter of her Son."[1]

Elsewhere in the Tradition, Mary is a "garden enclosed," watered by the Stream of Living Waters. Not only is she mother, but she is the Virgin Mother, a garden *enclosed*, and her son is both truly her son and the Son of God.

PRAYER HANDS

Finally, we should notice that Mary is lost in prayer for much of our lectio! We have placed her in the posture with which she appears at places like Fatima and Kibeho, her hands folded in prayer at her breast, fingers to the sky. She is truly at one with God, a summary of the Good News flowing together as a song in her soul.

Christ is the summation of our whole human history, even of those things that we have not yet been able to see and hear. Christ makes all things new (see 2 Corinthians 5:17). We glimpse this in Mary with this lectio. As the novelist Thomas Howard once wrote, Christ "restore[s] the symphonies and operas" we have yet to hear! And all the beauty we have yet to behold.[2]

PRAY WITH LECTIO DIVINA

"Jesus." Mary was surprised by the sound of her own voice. She had but whispered his name, her lips barely touching his soft, velvety ear. Yet, as the name fell from her lips, it resounded within her. It became a rich melody reverberating within, mothering a heavenly love in the deepest recesses of her being. This was her son, and *she* was his mother.

Jesus looked at his mother, fully awake. His eyes were dark as freshly tilled earth, iridescent under a warm sun; his mouth a shell-pink bud.

"Jesus!" She spoke his name aloud, to herself and to Joseph, as she handed Jesus to him. Joseph took Mary's son in his arms and caressed his rosy cheek with his strong, work-worn hand. "Jesus." The heavenly feeling within Mary's soul grew, longing to nurture the shell-pink bud into a blossom of words: "Mama!"

Again, her voice was new, sounding to the ears of her heart like a whole chorus and choir of melodies. Many voices were speaking at one with hers, converging upon the name "Jesus."

First came Joseph's voice, hushed and low, strong and protective. Then, cascading over and around Joseph's "Jesus" was the voice of scripture, "like many waters" whispering: "The LORD make his face shine upon you, and be gracious to you!" Over top of scripture's rush, Mary heard the angel Gabriel's luminous song: "Behold, you will conceive in your womb and bear a son, and you shall call his name Jesus." And, finally, in response, Mary perceived the clear sound of Elizabeth's joy joining the chorus: "Blessed are you among women, and blessed is the fruit of your womb!" The song rose and rose, like fiery light within her.

Mary clasped her hands together on her breast, with her fingers pointed to the sky. Words she knew well poured forth in her own voice: "Behold[:] the handmaid of the Lord! My soul magnifies the Lord, and my spirit rejoices in God my Savior, for he has regarded the low estate of his handmaiden!"

In truth, to anyone listening, the cave was silent, but for the voices of Mary and Joseph exchanging the name of Jesus, unspoken except by the angel Gabriel, until now. The symphony within Mary was the same feeling of joy that had taken hold of her soul at the garden well, life-giving water and light flowing through every fiber of her being. She was a mother, and *this* was her son!

The shell-pink mouth stretched into a yawn, as did the baby's whole body, loosely swaddled from chin to toe, except for the tiny hand with tiny fingers curled around the edge of Joseph's cloak. Mary reached again for Jesus, and taking him back into her arms, she laid him at her breast.

His eyes of earth looked up at her, growing sleepy with milk.

CONTEMPLATE WITH VISIO DIVINA

Gaze at this painting for a few minutes. What things catch your attention? What do you notice first, and why? Take in every detail—the colors, light, depiction of the created world. What emotions and insights well up in you?

FOLLOW MARY TODAY

We offer here not a single saint, but, fittingly, a whole chorus. Let us see and hear how Mary has been beheld by the visionaries who experienced such a singular privilege with the eyes of flesh. We will see that Mary is announcing herself not just as the Mother of God, but in virtue of such a title, as our mother, too.

We begin with St. Juan Diego. Our Lady appeared to St. Juan Diego during the Advent season of 1531. She was so radiant, the whole earth surrounding her appeared like gems and jewels, shining and beautiful, flashing like gold. When Juan Diego first encountered Our Lady on Tepeyac Hill that Advent, she told him, "I am the Ever-virgin Holy Mary, Mother of the God of Great Truth." She charged Juan Diego with a mission: "I very much want and ardently desire that my hermitage be erected in this place. In it I will show and give to all people all my love . . ."[3] Mary asked for a "home" amongst the Nahuatl people, to whom Juan belonged, precisely to show them her love.

Later, when Juan Diego was avoiding Mary because he was anxious about his ailing uncle, Mary found him and said, "Am I not here, your mother?" With these moving words, Mary reiterated her motherly presence to Juan Diego. She continued, saying: "Are you not under my shadow and my protection? Am I not your source of life? Are you not in the hollow of my mantle where I cross my arms? Who else do you need?"[4] With these words, Mary invited Juan Diego, and all of us, into the "hollow" of Mary's mantle. There, as at Christmastime, we will always behold the even more wonderful sight: her son, Jesus.

Let us now travel to Lourdes, France, where on a clear and crisp February day Our Lady appeared to St. Bernadette Soubirous in 1858. Despite the cold, young Bernadette was sitting at the edge of an icy stream, removing her socks and shoes. She meant to cross through the icy water to search for dry firewood to light and warm the forsaken Lourdes *cachot* that was her family's home. And that is when it happened. Sitting with one sock on, one sock off, Bernadette was startled to see Our Lady, Mary—the Mother of God!—appear in the grotto at Massabielle.

How very ordinary: Bernadette, half barefoot, a dirty stocking in hand, seeks warmth and light for her home. And yet, how astonishingly extra-ordinary: to find oneself so suddenly in the presence of such beauty—beauty beyond compare. And Bernadette is consumed by the sight, enraptured. The famous novel, *The Song of Bernadette*, describes Mary's appearance:

> A very young lady, delicate and dainty, visibly of flesh and blood, short rather than tall . . . stands calmly and without touching the side or arch in the narrow oval of the niche. The very young lady's garb is not at all common . . . her snow-white raiment is so cut as to indicate her delicate waistline. . . . Sometimes [her dress] gleams like satin or silk, sometimes it is duller, like some unknown, very delicate ineffably snowy velvet; again it seems like a transparently thin batiste that transmits to its folds every stirring of the limbs. . . . Wavy ringlets of her light brown hair escape from under the veil. A quite broad blue girdle lightly knotted under the breast, falls down over the knee. But what a blue! Lovely to the point of pain. . . . Bernadette observes the most striking thing last of all: the young lady's feet are bare. And the tiny narrow feet give the effect of ivory, almost of alabaster. . . . The strangest thing, however, is this: two golden roses are placed . . . at the slender toes of each foot . . . Bernadette would like to speak, to burst out in

> words or even in inarticulate songs, stammering, reverential, tender.[5]

The beauty of the mother, as beheld by Bernadette, is the beauty of God-with-us. This is what we long to see! Indeed, this beauty holds Bernadette for the rest of her life. It is the simple but gripping reality of Mary's compassionate motherhood that is made visible to Bernadette. It was a compassion she never knew, until that moment, that she needed to experience, to know, and to be enraptured with, always.

The "incomparable beauty" of the Mother of God is corroborated by other visionaries. The children of Fatima, for example, tell us of Mary's beauty. There, she appeared to be "bright as the sun" and spoke with a melodious voice. Alphonsine Mumureke, one of the visionaries at Kibeho (in Rwanda), tells us, "Her skin shines like polished ivory. . . . All I can say about her appearance is that she is more beautiful than anyone or anything on the planet; I don't have words to describe such beauty."[6] And her voice was "soothing," "lyrical," and heavenly.[7] Sr. Agnes of Akita, Japan, joins the chorus: When Mary spoke to her, a "voice of indescribable beauty . . . of a beauty without limit," struck her "totally deaf ears."[8] A "symphony" never before heard!

Beholding Mary, the Mother of God *and our mother*, with these visionaries might just draw us into song ourselves, "stammering, reverential, tender." Beholding Mary, we could sing with her: "My soul magnifies the Lord, and my spirit rejoices in God my Savior!" For in her we see her son, "Jesus," the God who saves us with love.

EIGHT

BEHOLD OUR KING

SOLEMNITY OF THE EPIPHANY

PREPARE THE WAY

If the Solemnity of Mary, Holy Mother of God is like a second annunciation, Epiphany is a second Christmas. Trumpeted abroad by the Christmas star, Christ's birth is announced to the Magi, three wise kings *from the East*. The kings travel from afar to worship this newborn king. The Christmas star and the worship of the Magi represent the revelation of the Christ Child to all the nations on Epiphany.

Accordingly, the scriptures for Epiphany invite us to *Arise [and] shine*, for our light has come: the glory of the Lord shines upon [us] . . . and *his glory is seen upon [us]!*

With these words, scripture speaks of both the Christmas star (*over us appears his glory*) and the infant Christ (*the glory of the Lord shines upon us*). *Rising up*, we take a closer look at the child in Mary's arms, contemplating him in the marvelous light of Christmas, as our Lord and our God.

With the Magi, then, we encounter Mary's baby as our king. The wondrous beholding of Christmas morning becomes the wondrous praise and thanksgiving of Epiphany. Our gazing becomes worship.

Mary observes the grateful beholding of the Magi. She witnesses their transformative sacrifice. After all, until now *they* were the ones being called "king." Yet, the Magi gladly exchange the treasures of their kingdoms for a single look at the Christ Child. The child's gaze was truly all they desired in return.

To the Magi, Christ's gaze was the supreme gift, and it was extended to them in Mary's arms. On Epiphany, Mary wraps the Christ Child in her arms and offers him to the world under the light of the Christmas star. She extends her son to us, so that we, too, may do him homage and be changed by such praise and thanksgiving. If we truly remain gazing upon him, looking into his eyes, we will find the King of Kings, our Lord and God. Transfixed and transformed by his gaze, we offer ourselves, like Mary, to a life that is all thanksgiving and praise, self-gift in exchange for self-gift.

BEHOLD THE WORD

ISAIAH 60:1–6

Arise, shine; for your light has come,
  and the glory of the LORD has risen upon you.
For behold, darkness shall cover the earth,

and thick darkness the peoples;
but the LORD *will arise upon you,*
and his glory will be seen upon you.
And nations shall walk by your light,
and kings in the brightness of your rising.
Lift up your eyes round about, and see;
they all gather together, they come to you;
your sons shall come from afar,
and your daughters shall be carried in the arms.
Then you shall see and be radiant;
your heart shall thrill and rejoice,
because the abundance of the sea shall be turned
to you,
the wealth of the nations shall come to you.
A multitude of camels shall cover you,
the young camels of Mid'ian and E'phah;
all those from Sheba shall come.
They shall bring gold and frankincense,
and shall proclaim the praise of the LORD.

MATTHEW 2:1–12

Now when Jesus was born in Bethlehem of Judea in the days of Herod the king, behold, Wise Men from the East came to Jerusalem, saying, "Where is he who has been born king of the Jews? For we have seen his star in the East, and have come to worship him." When Herod the king heard this, he was troubled, and all Jerusalem with him; and assembling all the chief priests and scribes of the people, he inquired of them where the Christ was to be born. They told him, "In Bethlehem of Judea; for so it has been written by the prophet:

> *'And you, O Bethlehem, in the land of Judah,*
> *are by no means least among the rulers of Judah;*
> *for from you shall come a ruler*
> *who is to shepherd my people Israel.'"*

Then Herod summoned the Wise Men secretly and ascertained from them what time the star appeared; and he sent them to Bethlehem, saying, "Go and search diligently for the child, and when you have found him bring me word, that I too may come and worship him." When they had heard the king, they went their way; and, behold, the star which they had seen in the East went before them, till it came to rest over the place where the child was. When they saw the star, they rejoiced exceedingly with great joy; and going into the house, they saw the child with Mary his mother, and they fell down and worshiped him. Then, opening their treasures, they offered him gifts, gold and frankincense and myrrh. And being warned in a dream not to return to Herod, they departed to their own country by another way.

CONSIDER THE SCENE

We find Christ at the center of our lectio for Epiphany, folded in his mother's arms. Indeed, the primary image of our lectio is that of an exchange or an embrace. In the central paragraphs, Christ beholds the Magi from within the embrace of his mother's arms, while the Magi offer him treasures in exchange for a single glance from his dove-like eyes.

THE WONDROUS EXCHANGE

This is no commercial exchange. It is, rather, a profound exchange of love. We find it described in the Song of Solomon this way: *You have ravished my heart . . . with a glance of your eyes, with one jewel of your necklace* (Song of Solomon 4:9).

The central image and structure of our lectio are both borrowed from one of our most ancient Christmas antiphons, "O, Marvelous Exchange!"

> *O marvelous exchange!*
> *Man's Creator has become man, born of a virgin.*
> *We have been made sharers in the divinity of Christ*
> *who humbled himself to share in our humanity.*[1]

This antiphon sings so well of Christmas that even the very structure of its lines imitates the marvelous exchange of the Incarnation. See, for example, how the second line begins with God (Man's Creator) and ends with us (the Virgin Mary), and then the third line begins with us and ends with God, and then, in the final line, we begin again with God (who humbled himself) and end with "our humanity." Thus, the antiphon quite literally draws us into the center of God's embrace while we are singing these words, line by line. Singing this antiphon, our praise *is* an embrace!

PRAISE AS SELF-GIFT

Singing about the "Marvelous Exchange," we enter more deeply into Christmas. Will we passively observe this newborn babe, or will we enter into an exchange of love with God, "who humbled himself to share in our humanity"?

Mary is the first and best example of accepting this invitation from God. She is our sure guide. On Epiphany, her yes is echoed by the Magi. Their wondrous beholding is, like Mary's beholding, an exchange of gifts, one self for another. The mutual gift of one self for another is our truest form of praise and thanksgiving. It is an act of pure love. God has called us to nothing less, and he offers nothing less to us himself. On Epiphany, God calls us through the star, as he called the Magi: Lay your crowns before the Christ Child. In their act of casting down their crowns, the Magi declared that homage was no longer due to them, but, rather, to this infant, asleep in his mother's arms. The journey of the Magi was their fiat both to their death as kings and to their life with God. We are called to join in their thanksgiving and praise, and so join our lives with God, too.

KING HEROD REFUSES THE STAR

King Herod stands in stark contrast to the Magi. Our lectio gestures toward the likes of King Herod in the shadowy chattering of black starlings.[2] Quite disingenuously, Herod ordered the Magi to "Go and search diligently for the child, and when you have found him bring me word, that I too may come and worship him" (Mt 2:8). Herod intended no such thing! Frightened by a sleeping baby, Herod sought to kill the Christ Child, casting a black shadow against the brilliance of the Christmas star.

Finally, as troubling as Herod's death designs are, they are also part of Epiphany's brilliant light—the Christmas star continues to shine despite Herodian shadows. God truly became a baby. And just like any other baby, he was innocent and helpless. God put himself at the mercy of a mother's arms and a father's tender care.

ST. IGNATIUS'S STAR

Mary and her mothering arms are part of the Christmas star's "trumpet-tongued secrets," as they were called by St. Ignatius of Antioch.[3] St. Ignatius once wrote a letter to the faithful at

Ephesus, quite fitting for Epiphany. We close this lectio commentary with Ignatius's words:

> "Mary's virginity was hidden from the prince of this world; so was her child-bearing . . . these three trumpet-tongued secrets were brought to pass in the deep silence of God. How, then, were they made known to the world? Up in the heavens a star gleamed out. . . . God was now appearing in human form to bring in a new order, even life without end."[4]

PRAY WITH LECTIO DIVINA

Earlier that evening, Mary watched as black starlings winged through the beaming starlight. The birds whirled and swirled through the night air, swift and sudden, wing to wing. In a shadowy flash, the whole chattering darted toward the branches of a nearby almond tree, and settled there, in gregarious, chirping conversation.

A similarly sudden arrival of three kings, *from the East*, now occupied Mary's attention. The same beaming starlight streamed through the stable's rough-hewn door and alighted in glints and glimmers on the kings' three golden crowns. They had come, they said, to do homage to the baby Jesus, drawing near to Mary in swishing silken robes and splendid coats. She breathed in the beautiful scent of aromatic spices.

As they knelt before her child, their crowns fell to the ground and went rolling across the stone floor. What a melodious clanging! The crowns came to rest between the feet of the ox and the ass. And there they stayed, never to be taken up again.

Mary observed the three bare heads of the Magi, bent low to the ground and inches from her own feet. The sound of their voices rose slowly to her ears: a low, swelling sound, "Alleluia, Alleluia, Alleluia!" And then they said, with evident excitement: "We saw his star in the East and have come to worship him. The star, that trumpet of light, rose and led us here with silent, glittering speech: Come! He is here! In Bethlehem! A babe in the arms of his mother; a ruler, who is to shepherd the Nations."

Awoken by the clanging commotion, the babe in Mary's arms gazed steadily at these three kings, with eyes *like doves* (Sg 1:15; 4:1).

Gazing upon the babe, the kings *rejoiced exceedingly with great joy*. They opened their *treasures and offered* him *gifts, gold and frankincense and myrrh*. With their heads again bent low and their arms outstretched, the Magi offered an even greater gift than all their royal treasures. They offered him true worship in the thrilled throbbing of their hearts.

And, then, as suddenly and joyfully as the kings had come, they went. They cut a straight line across the shepherds' fields, casting tall silhouettes from atop their camels and carrying new treasures: the memory of a mother's arms and a babe with eyes *like doves*. As the Magi passed under the almond tree, the chattering of starlings burst into the sky—a dark, murmuring constellation against the bright night sky. Mary and Joseph watched in silence as the kings grew smaller and smaller against the horizon . . . and disappeared.

No one else came. Not Caesar. Not Quirinius. Nor Herod, who didn't even have far to travel! And yet the star-beams trumpeted more brightly than ever—brighter, even, than the fullest moon! Mary, herself radiant, sat amidst the brilliance of the star and the brilliance of her child. It was as Isaiah said it would be:

> *The LORD will arise upon [us],*
> *and his glory will be seen upon [us].*
> *And nations shall walk by your light, [my Son,]*
> *and kings in the brightness of your rising!*

CONTEMPLATE WITH VISIO DIVINA

Gaze at this painting for a few minutes. What things catch your attention? What do you notice first, and why? Take in every detail—the colors, light, depiction of the created world. What emotions and insights well up in you?

FOLLOW MARY TODAY

> Virgin mother, daughter of your son,
> more humble and sublime than any creature . . .
> you are the one who gave to human nature
> so much nobility that its Creator
> did not disdain his being made its creature.[5]

Thus Dante Alighieri opens the third installment of his *Divine Comedy*, the *Paradiso*. He praises Mary by echoing the Christmas antiphon, "O, Marvelous Exchange!" It is as if he says, "Thank you, Mary, for the Incarnation. Thank you for my way back to God!"

Dante confesses that he was once lost in a "Dark Wood," beset by sin, and lacking the light of faith to find "the path that does not stray." The experience, he tells us, was "so bitter—death is hardly more severe!"[6]

Within this "dense and difficult" Dark Wood, Mary came to lead Dante toward the stars of heaven. With Mary as our guide, Dante says, we can "climb unto [those] stars," rising with each step toward "the Love that moves the sun and the other stars."[7] Mary's succor, as Dante attests, fans even the smallest "spark" of faith "to vivid flame, and, like a star in heaven, [our faith can grow] sparkling" within us.[8]

Like the Magi heeding the Christmas star, Dante followed Mary. His gratitude for the grace-filled journey of faith pours forth from his mouth and his pen as poetry: a gift of praise for Mary's son, the Living Light, sparkling now within him.

NOTES

1. BEHOLD THE INCARNATION: AS ADVENT BEGINS

1. Bernard of Clairvaux, "Homily IV," *Homilies in Praise of the Blessed Virgin Mary*, trans. Marie-Bernard Said (Cistercian Publications, 1993), iv, 7.

2. Takashi Nagai, *Thoughts from Nyokodo*, trans. Gabriele Comice (Amici Nagai, 2023), 47.

2. BEHOLD CHRIST OUR HOPE: FIRST SUNDAY OF ADVENT

1. Gerard Manley Hopkins, "Mary as Compared to the Air We Breathe," International Hopkins Association, published December 10, 2018, updated July 26, 2024, accessed March 13, 2025, https://hopkinspoetry.com/poem/the-blessed-virgin/.

2. Ibid.

3. St. Ephrem, "Hymns on the Nativity," *Mary and the Fathers of the Church: The Blessed Virgin Mary in Patristic Thought*, trans. Luigi Gambero (Yale University Press, 2016), 112.

4. St. Ephrem, "Hymns on the Church," *Mary and the Fathers*, 116.

5. Gustavo Ponce, "St. Laura Montoya in the Missionary Vanguard of the Church," *Catholic Magazine*, October 2013, accessed December 1, 2024, https://catholicmagazine.news/st-laura-montoya-in-the-missionary-vanguard-of-the-church/.

3. BEHOLD CHRIST OUR PEACE: SECOND SUNDAY OF ADVENT

1. Takashi Nagai, *The Pass of the Virgin: A History of the Martyrs of Tsuwano*, trans. Gabriele Comice (Amici Nagai, 2024), 53–54.

4. BEHOLD CHRIST OUR JOY: THIRD SUNDAY OF ADVENT

1. St. Francis of Assisi, "Salutation of the Blessed Virgin Mary," in *Francis and Clare: The Complete Works*, trans. Regis Armstrong, O.F.M. Cap. and Ignatius C. Brady, O.F.M. (Paulist Press, 1982), 149–150.

2. Pope Francis, "Apostolic Letter *Admirabile Signum* of the Holy Father Francis on the Meaning and Importance of the Nativity Scene," section 5, The Holy See, December 1, 2019, accessed December 1, 2024, https://www.vatican.va/content/francesco/en/apost_letters/documents/papa-francesco-lettera-ap_20191201_admirabile-signum.html.

3. Pope Francis, *Admirabile Signum*, section 1.

5. BEHOLD CHRIST OUR LOVE: FOURTH SUNDAY OF ADVENT

1. Thérèse of Lisieux, *Story of a Soul*, trans. John Beevers (Doubleday, 2010), 10.

2. Thérèse of Lisieux, *Story*, 23.

3. Thérèse of Lisieux, *Story*, 10.

4. Thérèse of Lisieux, *Story*, 19-20.

5. Thérèse of Lisieux, *Story*, 34.

6. Thérèse of Lisieux, *Story*, 3.

7. BEHOLD OUR MOTHER: SOLEMNITY OF MARY, THE HOLY MOTHER OF GOD

1. Dante Alighieri, "*Paradiso* 33," 1–6, Digital Dante, published in partnership with Columbia University Libraries, accessed November 9, 2024, https://digitaldante.columbia.edu/dante/divine-comedy/paradiso/paradiso-33/.

2. Thomas Howard, *Christ the Tiger* (Ignatius Press, 1989), 151.

3. *Nican Mohopua in Guadalupe: Mother of the New Creation*, trans. Virgil Elizondo (Maryknoll: Orbis, 1997), 7–8.

4. *Nican Mohopua*, 16.

5. Franz Werfel, *Song of Bernadette* (Ignatius Press, 2006), 55–57.

6. Immaculée Ilibagiza, *Our Lady of Kibeho* (Hay House, 2008), 42.

7. Ilibagiza, *Kibeho*, 40.

8. Teiji Yasuda, *Akita: The Tears and Message of Mary*, trans. John M. Haffert (101 Foundation, 1989), 35.

8. BEHOLD OUR KING: SOLEMNITY OF THE EPIPHANY

1. "Antiphon of the first psalm for Evening Prayer I on the Solemnity of Mary, Mother of God," *The Liturgy of the Hours*, vol. 1 (Catholic Book Publishing, 1975), 477.

2. Dante Alighieri, "*Inferno* 5," Digital Dante, published in partnership with Columbia University Libraries, accessed November 9, 2024, https://digitaldante.columbia.edu/dante/divine-comedy/inferno/inferno-5/.

3. Ignatius of Antioch, "Letter to the Ephesians," in *Early Christian Writings: The Apostolic Fathers*, ed. Andrew Louth, trans. Maxwell Staniforth (Penguin, 1987), 19.

4. Ignatius, "Ephesians," 19.

5. Dante Alighieri, "*Paradiso* 33," 1–6, Digital Dante, published in partnership with Columbia University Libraries, accessed November 9, 2024, https://digitaldante.columbia.edu/dante/divine-comedy/paradiso/paradiso-33/.

6. Dante Alighieri, "*Inferno* 1," 1–7, Digital Dante, published in partnership with Columbia University Libraries, accessed November 9, 2024, https://digitaldante.columbia.edu/dante/divine-comedy/inferno/inferno-1/.

7. Dante, "*Paradiso* 33,"145.

8. Dante, "*Paradiso* 24," 145–147.

CATHERINE CAVADINI is a teaching professor and director of the master of arts program in theology at the University of Notre Dame. She teaches courses on the saints, scriptural interpretation, and Church history.

She earned a master's degree in theological studies from Duke University and a doctorate in theology from the University of Notre Dame.

Cavadini provided a theological review for the *Living the Word Catholic Women's Bible* and contributed a number of articles, including "Illuminating Fire: How Scripture Enlightens, Attracts, and Transforms." She is also cohost of the *Living the Word Catholic Women's Bible* companion videos.

Cavadini lives in South Bend, Indiana, with her husband and children.

ANASTASSIA CASSADY is a freelance artist and high school art teacher at Trinity Academy in South Bend, Indiana.

She studied art and art history at the University of Michigan and Indiana University.

Cassady has taken on many commissions, including church murals, altarpiece paintings, paschal candles, Byzantine icons, gilding a baldacchino, book covers, and oil paintings.

Instagram: @cassadytess
Facebook: @tess.godfrey.7

AVE

Ave Maria Press

Founded in 1865, Ave Maria Press, a ministry of the Congregation of Holy Cross, is a Catholic publishing company that serves the spiritual and formative needs of the Church and its schools, institutions, and ministers; Christian individuals and families; and others seeking spiritual nourishment.

For a complete listing of titles from

Ave Maria Press

Sorin Books

Forest of Peace

Christian Classics

visit www.avemariapress.com

AVE | Ave Maria Press
Notre Dame, IN
A Ministry of the United States Province of Holy Cross